M000022376

TIPS OF THE TONGUE

The Nonnative English Speaker's Guide to

MASTERING PUBLIC SPEAKING

Deborah Grayson Riegel
& Ellen Dowling

INDIE BOOKS
INTERNATIONAL

Copyright © 2017 Deborah Grayson Riegel & Ellen Dowling

All rights reserved.
Printed in the United States of America.

No part of this publication may be reproduced or distributed in any form or by any means, without the prior permission of the publisher. Requests for permission should be directed to permissions@indiebooksintl.com, or mailed to Permissions, Indie Books International, 2424 Vista Way, Suite 316, Oceanside, CA 92054.

Neither the publisher nor the author is engaged in rendering legal or other professional services through this book. If expert assistance is required, the services of an appropriate professional should be sought. The publisher and the author shall have neither liability nor responsibility to any person or entity with respect to any loss or damage caused directly or indirectly by the information in this publication.

ISBN-10: 1-941870-88-0
ISBN-13: 978-1-941870-88-4
Library of Congress Control Number: 2017937162

Designed by Joni McPherson, mcphersongraphics.com
INDIE BOOKS INTERNATIONAL, LLC
2424 VISTA WAY, SUITE 316
OCEANSIDE, CA 92054
www.indiebooksintl.com

Dedicated to:

Michael, Jacob, and Sophie, my favorite around-the-world traveling companions.

Deborah Grayson Riegel

Xzavier Weldon, my beloved grandson, wishing you a future filled with joy and applause.

Ellen Dowling

Contents

A Message to Our Readers

D ozens of books provide instruction in how to improve your presentation skills. After all, public speaking is on most people's top ten list of things to avoid (and for some people, it's on their top one list). But for a growing subset of global business professionals—those who need to present in English when English isn't their native language—the anxiety related to speaking in public is even more pronounced. Considering the language barriers they need to overcome, the cultural norms they need to learn, and the general challenges associated with public speaking, nonnative English speakers have it harder than most.

This book makes it easier.

Tips of the Tongue: The Nonnative English Speaker's Guide to Mastering Public Speaking is a practical, tactical, and supportive how-to book aimed at addressing the unique problems that nonnative English speakers experience when they deliver a presentation in public.

This isn't an English-as-a-Second-Language (ESL) book, nor is it an accent-modification book. It's a tool kit to help reduce anxiety and increase the confidence, competence, and cultural comfort of those who have to present in English when English isn't their first language.

Based on our collective five decades of experience with teaching presentation skills to leaders—with several of those decades dedicated to working with nonnative English speaking leaders— this book captures the tips, tools, and techniques we've shared with our clients across the globe.

If any of the following are the case, this book is for you:

- English is your second (or third or fourth) language.

- Your job (or volunteer role/hobby) requires you to make presentations frequently.

- You experience anxiety when speaking in public, and your worries are worsened by the extra burden of having to speak in English.

- You feel like your English is pretty good—until you have to make a presentation in front of an audience.

- You are particularly uncomfortable speaking in front of a Western audience.

- You are afraid that you'll say the wrong thing, gesture inappropriately, or bore the audience.

- You worry that your struggle to present in English will undermine the message you are trying to get across.

What if you're reading this and your first language *is* English? Keep reading. If you could use a refresher on how to structure your presentation, engage your audience, manage questions and answers (Q&A), and more, then you'll find a lot in here that's useful for you, too.

We, the authors, both speak only one primary language—English— and so we commend, respect, and admire those of you who have added this complex tongue to your repertoire. We know we would have plenty to learn from you.

Tips of the Tongue: The Nonnative English Speaker's Guide to Mastering Public Speaking is what you can learn from us.

—Deborah Grayson Riegel and Ellen Dowling

The Key Behaviors of (Almost) All Successful Presenters

Be sincere, be brief, be seated.

UNITED STATES PRESIDENT FRANKLIN D. ROOSEVELT

oosevelt's recommendation is smart advice for any presenter, whether English is your first, second, third, or tenth language. The most successful presenters speak from their hearts, get to the point, and wrap it up before the audience gets bored or overwhelmed. Of course, this is usually easier said than done. Before we get into specific detail about how to make an effective presentation in English, we think it would be very helpful to review the common characteristics of effective presentations in general. Here are ten behaviors exhibited by the most successful presenters in *any* culture:

1. They deliver a message with credibility and sincerity. No matter what the actual topic is, most presentations are persuasive; the goal of the presentation is to convince the audience of the validity and value of what you are presenting to them. (Even if you are presenting an informational status report, you want your audience to believe that the details you are providing are both true and useful.)

Therefore, it is critical that the audience buys in to your main points.

In no other media of communication is the person delivering the information as important as the message itself. If the audience does not believe in *you*, they're not going to believe in your ideas. A good example of this is a medical professional who hosts a TV show about new advances in medicine. Even though this doctor may be selling products that have no real medicinal value (and no scientific support to back up their health claims), if the doctor comes across to the audience as believable, credible, and sincere, people will line up to buy the product. The same holds true in reverse: If the doctor appears to be a quack or a phony, the audience will have nothing to do with what he or she is selling, even if the products are actually effective.

Never doubt that the messenger is equally as important as the message.

If you want to get across an idea, wrap it up in a person.

NOBEL PEACE PRIZE WINNER RALPH BUNCHE

---

2. They speak in a way that is easy to understand. It goes without saying that if the audience cannot understand you, they're not going to get much out of your presentation. If you speak too quietly and they can't hear you, or if you speak too loudly and hurt their ears, or if you speak too quickly and they can't keep up, or if you speak too slowly and they begin to doze off, you will be wasting everyone's time—and the opportunity to make an impact. There are many ways to improve your vocal skills and overcome the challenges posed by an accent unfamiliar to your audience's ears. However, it's not the audience's job to make sense of your presentation. It's yours.

The noblest pleasure is the joy of understanding.
LEONARDO DA VINCI

3. They clearly explain the benefits of the presentation.
Audience members need to know "what's in it for me?" if they attend your presentation. You need to know the answer to the question, "Why should my audience care about this?" And then you need to figure out a way to present the answer early in your presentation. You can do this only if you have done your homework and have tried to understand your audience's point of view. Ask yourself these questions: "Who are they? Why are they here? What do they already know about my subject? What will they want to learn?" In short, you need to understand your audience before you can know what will most appeal to them.

Pretend that every single person you meet has a sign around his or her neck that says, "Make me feel important." Not only will you succeed in sales, you will succeed in life.
BUSINESSWOMAN MARY KAY ASH

4. They adapt their own personal style to meet the needs of the audience. Every culture has preferences for what makes successful communication. Some cultures prefer that speakers get to the point quickly, cite only the relevant facts, then sum up and close. Others prefer that speakers build up to a conclusion gradually, piece by piece, to allow listeners time to process the argument before being

3

confronted with the main point. Some like lots of stories to paint vivid pictures in their minds; others want just the facts and consider stories a waste of valuable time. Which kind of audience are you speaking to and how will you adjust your own personal preferences to meet their specific needs?

A personal style is like handwriting—it happens as the byproduct of our way of seeing things, enriched by the experiences of everything around us.
ITALIAN DESIGNER MASSIMO VIGNELLI

5. They honor the given time limits. When asked to speak for a certain amount of time, an effective speaker takes great care not to go over the time limit, as this can be frustrating for audiences as well as discourteous to any other presenters who may be speaking next. In order to fit your presentation into a specific amount of time, you need to structure your talk very carefully, being aware of places where you might want to expand on a point or places where your audience might want to insert a comment or a question.

It becomes even trickier if the speaker before you greatly exceeded his or her time limit, cutting into your speaking time. If you insist on sticking with your agreed-upon time, you run the risk of alienating your audience members, who know very well what time it is and how much time is left.

Take a tip from the playwright George Bernard Shaw, who once found himself to be the last speaker in an evening when the speakers before him had each gone significantly over their allotted time. When his turn came, Shaw stood up and said, "Ladies and gentlemen, the subject is not exhausted, but we are." And he sat back down.

Right time, right place, right people equals success. Wrong time, wrong place, wrong people equals most of the real human history.

SUFI AUTHOR AND TEACHER IDRIES SHAH, REFLECTIONS

---

6. They know how to use technology skillfully. If you're going to use PowerPoint, Keynote, or any other visual presentation program, you must learn how to use it seamlessly and effectively, and you must practice, practice, practice until you know the order of the slides backwards and forwards. Nothing looks more unprofessional than a presenter who clicks to the next slide, then is surprised to see what it is. Whether you're making a slide presentation, showing a video clip, playing music, speaking into a microphone or anything else with a power connection, you need to show mastery over the technology to support your credibility. Of course, even if you're taking a low-tech approach (such as writing on flip charts or a white board), you want to be mindful of using the tools skillfully, thoughtfully, and yes, legibly.

People who know what they're talking about don't need PowerPoint.

STEVE JOBS

---

7. They have a back-up plan in case things go wrong. Have you heard of Murphy's Law? It states, "Anything that can go wrong will go wrong." The wise presenter imagines many different scenarios where the presentation can fall apart: Your laptop decides to die during your presentation; the slide program you're using is not compatible with the provided system; your slides are unreadable due to the lighting in the room; there is a power outage; you can't find your notes; your audience is much larger (or much smaller) than you were anticipating; the decision-maker is late; there's construction going on outside—these are all situations that we have personally experienced and survived. If you can imagine something going wrong, rest assured that it has gone wrong before and probably will again. The solution: Prepare for the worst, hope for the best, and build enough rapport and trust with your audience that a glitch or two won't undermine your personal or professional credibility.

Murphy was an optimist.
AN EXPERIENCED PRESENTER

---

8. They prepare thoroughly (without memorizing everything).
An excellent presenter does not memorize the presentation. For one thing, a presentation may last several hours or more, and who could possibly memorize a three-hour speech (unless you're playing the part of Hamlet)? For another, memorizing will result in your presentation sounding forced, phony, or like an insincere actor. And what if a bird flies by the window and disrupts your concentration? What if you need to change direction after an audience member asks a pointed question? Memorization gets in the way of interpersonal connection and flexibility. It also tends to cause more anxiety than it alleviates.

Excellent presenters speak from notes that remind them of their main points and the sequence of those points. And they know their topic so well and have rehearsed their talk so thoroughly that the audience is often not aware that they are using notes at all.

Your goal is "rehearsed spontaneity." With enough practice, you can help your audience experience (as the great Russian acting teacher Konstantin Stanislavsky put it) "the illusion of the first time." And with enough preparation, you will be able to shift and adapt along the way.

The measure of intelligence is the ability to change.
ALBERT EINSTEIN

---

9. They engage the audience and avoid lecturing them. To be an excellent presenter, you need to resist the urge to do *all* the talking. There are many ways to involve your audience in your presentation, from simple survey questions ("How many of you feel that you spend too much time on your mobile phone?"), to checks for understanding ("And that's what makes it so effective. What questions do you have?"), to telling stories, to using analogies and examples, to including pictures of members of your audience in your slide show. (Dr. Jonathan Dowling, Ellen's quantum physicist brother, uses this technique in his scientific presentations.)

Presenters who treat a speech like a one-way street risk losing the audience's engagement, involvement, and attention. Presenters who take a two-way-street approach to public speaking invite connection, trust, and buy-in.

I hear, and I forget; I see, and I remember;
I do and I understand.
CHINESE PROVERB

10. They move purposefully. There are two kinds of ineffective presenters: those who move too little and those who move too much. Move too little and your audience will grow tired and bored. Move too much and your audience will experience you as nervous and unfocused. The goal is to be somewhere in the middle, where your gestures punctuate your points and your movements make a statement.

The best presenters do not hide behind the lectern, which then becomes a barrier between the presenter and the audience. They approach their audiences, encouraging them to join in the presentation; they also move close to their visual aids to illustrate their points.

"Proxemics" is a scientific term for how your position in the space can affect the dynamics of your communication with your audience. When you change the usual proxemics (you step out from behind the lectern, for example), you immediately gain the audience's attention.

I move, therefore I am.
JAPANESE WRITER HARUKI MURAKAMI, 1Q84

Now that we have reviewed the key characteristics of an excellent presenter in any culture, let's see what techniques will help you deal with the specific problems that come from making a presentation in your second (or third or fourth) language.

Chapter 2

Overcoming Unique Challenges for Nonnative English Speakers

We're all islands shouting lies to each other across seas of misunderstanding.

RUDYARD KIPLING, THE LIGHT THAT FAILED

For nonnative English speakers, the feeling Kipling describes—being misunderstood—is even more pronounced, even when you're clearly speaking the truth.

We surveyed some of our international clients and colleagues to learn what specific challenges they faced when they attempted to make a presentation in English, and their responses can be boiled down into three overarching concerns: confidence, competence, and cultural comfort.

One professional who speaks Hebrew, Spanish, and English described several problems, including being self-conscious about her "weird and funny" accent (which seemed to get heavier the more nervous she became). She also told us how distracting it was to be aware of her grammar mistakes and how hard it was to be as spontaneous as she was in her native language. When this leader gave a presentation in English, she said she often felt somewhat powerless and "less smart."

A native Chinese speaker echoed these thoughts: "It is a very difficult task if you are not familiar with the content and you have to constantly recall what you are going to say in another language and at the same time come up with adequate grammar and wording."

Another Chinese speaker added that it's hard to express ideas appropriately. "When I can't find the word I need, I grasp the easiest word instead. So, a disaster would be like saying 'you guys' at a formal conference."

A Korean speaker was even more pessimistic: "I think one will be good at delivering what one prepared, but if the presentation goes beyond this scope, the situation will turn one's brain to mush and the disaster will begin."

A French speaker shared this perspective: "Speaking in public has always been a struggle. This may come from the school system because, if you hadn't done your homework, your punishment was to present something to the class and you were put in the spotlight. French people are amazed and impressed how at ease Americans are in presenting." (The authors would like to note that the majority of the American clients they have worked with don't feel "at ease" with presenting, despite the perception nonnative speakers might have.)

The challenges highlighted in these client examples are supported by research. In her *Harvard Business Review* article, "Global Business Speaks English," Harvard Business School associate professor Tsedal Neeley reports: "When nonnative speakers are forced to communicate in English, they can feel that their worth to the company has been diminished, regardless of their fluency level."[1]

---

[1] Neeley, Tsedal. "Global Business Speaks English." *Harvard Business Review.* July 31, 2014. Accessed February 21, 2017. https://hbr.org/2012/05/global-business-speaks-english.

In her team's interview of 164 employees at a German technology company two years after implementing an English-only policy, they found that nearly 70 percent of employees continued to experience frustration with it. At another firm based in France, 56 percent of medium-fluency English speakers and 42 percent of low-fluency speakers reported worrying about job advancement because of their relatively limited English skills.

As we know, anxiety about public speaking is pervasive regardless of language, country, or culture. But when you add to it the additional concerns of being a nonnative English speaker—and what that can mean for your career advancement when presenting in English is a job requirement—the pressure can feel overwhelming and the process disheartening. As Neeley reported, it's natural for non-English speakers to think: "I don't really feel like myself when I'm speaking English. I can only express a very small part of what I'm feeling."

Neeley advises patience, perspective, and reassurance to help nonnative speakers get a grip on the challenges of communicating in English. Here are five additional strategies to help you feel less lost when it comes to presenting in English:

1. **Prepare, prepare, and prepare your presentation some more.** Since it is so difficult to be spontaneous in a language that is not native to you, you can calm your nerves and boost your confidence by being absolutely sure that you know your material inside and out, upside down, and that you have rehearsed adequately and have considered what reaction you might have if things go wrong (which they frequently do). The late Steve Jobs, known for his captivating presentations,

put countless hours into rehearsing critical presentations that often had the whole world watching. He also demanded that outside speakers who were going to present to Apple audiences be practiced and polished to be in total control.

But being in total control of your presentation does not mean that you should either memorize what you are going to say or read your notes as though they were a movie script. Trying to deliver a memorized presentation will make you even *more* anxious, and you will look stiff and boring. Writing out your entire presentation and then reading it, word for word, to the audience (from your notes or from the slides) will usually alienate your audience and make them wish you had just e-mailed them the slides instead of forcing them to sit through an excruciatingly dull presentation. Think in an outline format, not a script format.

2. **Don't agonize about your accent.** Remember that you're not alone—everyone has an accent of some sort. Even people who live in different parts of one country can be identified by their accents. Your accent is part of who you are, and you should be proud of it.

An accent can be a problem for your audience, however, if they have difficulty understanding you. An unfamiliar accent is particularly problematic in the first minute or two or so of your presentation when your audience must initially strain to understand you. As your presentation continues, the problem becomes less acute as the audience will slowly develop an ear for your accent and find it easier to understand what you are saying. It can be helpful to include visuals in your opening statements so that the audience can see the context for your remarks and get the key points of your presentation as quickly as possible. There is an old saying that a picture is worth a thousand words. Indeed, showing the audience a picture of your main idea—using visual language—may fortify their initial understanding of your verbal language.

3. **If you can't think of the English word you need to make a point in your presentation, ask for help.** For example, if you're presenting on the topic of global warming, and you get stuck trying to remember the term "biodegradable," go ahead and ask the audience, "What's the term for substances that can be broken down by microorganisms?" Don't spend too much time scanning your memory for the right word—it will create an awkward scenario for your audience to watch your facial expressions shifting and twisting as you fight to retrieve the term you want. Just ask for what you need from the audience, which will give the audience the opportunity to engage with you.

Two other things to remember: First, you should already know in English and have practiced pronouncing the basic key terms associated with your topic. So, if your topic is global warming, you should be ready to retrieve from memory (or have written down in your notes) English words like "fossil fuels," "glaciers," and "greenhouse effect." Second, once the audience has shared a word or words with you, write it down. Audiences tend to be forgiving once, but if they need to rescue you repeatedly, your credibility will suffer, and your listeners will grow resentful.

4. *Slow down* to give your audience time to understand what you are saying. Just because you are fluent in English and can speak at a rapid pace, that doesn't mean you should do so in a presentation, especially at the beginning, when the audience needs time to get used to your manner of speaking. Choose your opening words deliberately and pronounce them carefully, being sure to articulate your words, not just rush through them.

According to their research in *Frontiers in Human Neuroscience*, authors Kristen J. Van Engen and Jonathan E. Peelle cite that audiences who are listening to accented speech of any kind experience "reductions in intelligibility, comprehensibility, and processing speed"[2] —the same effects caused by hearing loss or background noise. By slowing down your speaking pace, you help your audience to better manage the barriers to really hearing and understanding you.

Another technique that will help you slow down and give the audience time to catch up with your presentation is to pause frequently for effect (known as a *dramatic pause*). In the theater, the dramatic pause occurs when an actor maintains silence for a few seconds before saying or finishing a line, often to create suspense. Many polished public speakers use this technique to good effect as well. Examples include President Barack Obama, especially at the 2015 White House Correspondents Association Dinner[3]; Jack Ma, founder and CEO of Alibaba[4];

---

[2] Engen, Kristin J. Van, and Jonathan E. Peelle. "Listening Effort and Accented Speech." *Frontiers in Human Neuroscience* 8 (2014). doi:10.3389/fnhum.2014.00577.

[3] *President Obama at the 2015 White House Correspondents Dinner.* Performed by President Barack Obama. April 25, 2015. https://www.youtube.com/watch?v=NM6d06ALBVA.

Angela Merkel, President of Germany speaking to the British Parliament[5]; Chilean novelist Isabel Allende's TED Talk[6]; and Chinese businesswoman Yang Lan's TED Talk[7].

We cannot overstate the power of the pause for nonnative speakers. Van Engen and Peelle found that understanding accented speech requires listeners to draw on additional cognitive resources, not only to understand and remember what has been said but also to manage other information or tasks while listening to accented speech. Your pause is a gift to yourself and your listeners. For you, it gives you the opportunity to stop, consider what you want to say next, check your notes, read cues from the audience, or even take a sip of water. For your audience, it allows them to process what you're saying in a timely and relevant manner. You can also use a pause to build rapport with your audience by checking with them about your pace and pronunciation by saying something like, "Let me pause for a moment here. I know that I am making complete sense to myself in [Spanish/Hebrew/Japanese/Hindi/your native language]. How am I doing in English?" Not only will you likely get some immediate positive and supportive feedback from your audience, but you'll also be able to take a break, breathe, and gather your thoughts.

4 *Jack Ma: E-commerce in China and Around the World.* Performed by Jack Ma. March 20, 2013. https://www.youtube.com/watch?v=3OcNdxPhAUk.

5 *Angela Merkel Speaking English to British Parliament.* Performed by Angela Merkel. February 28, 2014. https://www.youtube.com/watch?v=cGZWR5S1lCo.

6 Allende, Isabel. "Tales of Passion." Isabel Allende: Tales of Passion | TED Talk | TED.com. Accessed February 23, 2017. http://www.ted.com/talks/isabel_allende_tells_tales_of_passion.

7 Lan, Yang. "The Generation That's Remaking China." Yang Lan: The Generation That's Remaking China | TED Talk | TED.com. Accessed February 23, 2017. http://www.ted.com/talks/yang_lan?language=en.

5. Remember that perfection is overrated. No one ever delivers a perfect presentation; everyone can make adjustments that will make the presentation better next time. In fact, a "perfect presentation" often sounds so scripted and polished that it lacks an emotional and personal connection with the audience.

In her book, *Presence,* Harvard Business School professor Amy Cuddy says that people judge us (and vice versa) on two dimensions, *warmth* and *competence.*[8] Most of us believe that competence is the more important factor, when, in fact, warmth is more critical. Indeed, competence is only evaluated once warmth (or trustworthiness) is established. A perfect presenter may exude credibility, but isn't likely to be experienced as warm or approachable. After all, who can relate to someone who is perfect? (We can't!)

And if you need some additional motivation, here's a quote from Idina Menzel, a singer most famous for her powerful soprano voice in such productions as *Wicked* (on Broadway) and *Frozen* (on film):

"There are about three million notes in a two-and-a-half-hour musical; being a perfectionist, it took me a long time to realize that if I'm hitting 75 percent of them, I'm succeeding. Performing isn't only about the acrobatics and the high notes: *It's staying in the moment, connecting with the audience in an authentic way, and making yourself real to them through the music.* I am more than

---

[8] Cuddy, Amy. *Presence: Bringing Your Boldest Self to Your Biggest Challenges.* St. Louis: Little, Brown, 2017.

the notes I hit, and that's how I try to approach my life. You can't get it all right all the time, but you can try your best. If you've done that, all that's left is to *accept your shortcomings and have the courage to try to overcome them.*"[9]

---

[9] Strecker, Erin. "Idina Menzel Defends Her New Year's Eve Performance: 'I Am More Than the Notes I Hit." *Billboard.* January 5, 2015. http://www.billboard.com/articles/news/6429348/idina-menzel-defends-new-years-eve-performance.

Chapter 3

Design a Strong Structure to Drive Success

Deep in the human unconscious is a pervasive need for a logical universe that makes sense.

NOVELIST FRANK HERBERT, DUNE

E ven if English is your native language, you won't be persuasive if your remarks are not logically organized. Most presenters get some degree of stage fright and therefore risk rambling if they don't have a clear and specific presentation plan. And if you're a nonnative English speaker, it is absolutely imperative that you use a structure that will provide a firm foundation for the presentation— one that will support your speech even as you might struggle with vocabulary, worry about proper usage, fret over your awkwardness, fuss over your illustrations—and still help you stay on point and focused.

The **Presentation Diamond** is one such structure that can help you design your presentation.

You see how easy it will be to design a well-shaped presentation by using the Presentation Diamond? At a glance, you can actually see the structure of your speech. All you have to do now is fill in the blanks.

How to do that? One method is to use small sticky notes to block out the first draft of your presentation. This approach allows you to change your mind, without having to rewrite anything. Here's how to do it:

1. Write a few key words about your opening, your objective, each of your main points, your recap, and your closing on individual sticky notes. Don't write sentences: Just write a few words that will enable you to remember the details later.

2. Place these notes in the appropriate places on a large board containing a sketch of the Presentation Diamond.

3. Determine if they are in the best possible order (especially the main points).

For example, if we were going to make a presentation on, say, "Why Seaweed Is Impractical for Stuffing Upholstery," we might devise sticky notes like these:

The comical story of the time we tried to stuff our couch with seaweed.

Three reasons why seaweed should not be used to stuff couches.

It tends to rot over time and smell bad.

It tends to seep through and turn your rug green.

Summary of the three reasons.

You need to collect an awful lot of seaweed.

Inspirational quote from Jacques Cousteau about seaweed.

Now, all we have to do is transfer these notes to the diamond. It should be fairly obvious which notes go where; the only decision we have left to make is in what order we should present the reasons:

1. The odor problem
2. The amount you need
3. The seepage problem

1. The amount you need
2. The odor problem
3. The seepage problem

1. The seepage problem
2. The odor problem
3. The amount you need

We will make our final decision based on our (vast) knowledge of the subject, as well as our understanding of what our audience will find most useful (depending on whether they're furniture upholsterers or deep-sea divers, for example).

You will notice that we assign separate sections at the top and the bottom of the Presentation Diamond for your opening and closing remarks. We believe that these should be listed separately from the objective and the summary because they perform such distinctive functions in a presentation.

Let's look at each part of the presentation in more detail.

Opening

The first thing you say must get your audience's attention. It must quiet them down if they've been chatting; it must energize them if they've been dozing. The first words out of your mouth will set the tone for your entire presentation; that's why so many people experience such severe stage fright in the first few minutes of a presentation. That is also why you must thoughtfully, carefully, and strategically prepare those first few minutes, especially if you are a nonnative speaker.

Here are five options for openings:

1. **Tell a story.** This story can be funny, heart-warming, surprising—you choose the mood you're trying to set—as long as it is relevant, engaging, and gets to the point quickly.

2. **State an impressive or surprising fact.** It should be something that captures your audience's attention by being novel and thought-provoking and, as always, relevant to the topic of the presentation.

   - "One out of every six people in this room will die of cancer."

   - "The federal government spent more money killing mosquitoes last year than you will earn in your lifetime."

   - "Banging your head against a wall burns 150 calories an hour."

3. **Ask the audience a question.** The question might call for an actual verbal response or a raised hand, or it can be rhetorical. No matter what kind of question you ask, it will prompt your listeners' brains to start engaging with you and the topic.

25

- "What part of this conference has been the highlight for you so far?"

- "How many of you have ever flown in a hot air balloon?"

- "Are you ever frustrated by delays in production caused by poor communication?"

4. **Give the audience something to do.** Just because you're the presenter, that doesn't mean you're the only one with something to do in that meeting. Get them involved right away. Have them write down an idea; fill out a survey; complete a handout; answer some questions with a partner or small group; etc. Giving the audience something to do early in the presentation also guarantees you a small but important break where you can check your notes, take a breath, have some water—whatever you need to do to recharge yourself for the rest of the presentation.

5. **Hold up an object.** This could be a prototype of your new product, an artifact from before your company's merger, or anything hard to identify. Ask people to guess what it is. Deborah worked with one speaker who held up a bottle of perfume that was the same scent worn by an elderly woman from the former Soviet Union he had met who was a beneficiary of his philanthropic organization. A little spray of the scent in the room further engaged his listeners and brought his topic to life.

Just remember, whatever you do, you must prepare this opening; you must not leave it to chance, nor can you treat it lightly. ("Well, um, good evening, it's an honor to be here, blah, blah, blah . . .") And whatever you do, don't open with an apology for something within your control. Ellen had the misfortune of being in the audience when the speaker began, "Well, I spent all week trying to come up with something to say tonight . . ." In contrast, Deborah was the speaker at a conference at which the power had gone out in the building, leaving the meeting room dark, the PowerPoint pointless, and the toilets unflushable. This was completely outside of her control, so she created a new opening to reference what everyone was experiencing. "As you know, today we're here to talk about collaboration. It's my job to shed some light on how you and your teams can work more effectively together. And, if I really do my job well, within a few hours, I'll also be able to shed some light on this ballroom, the hallways, and, most importantly, the bathrooms."

Objective

Immediately after your dynamic opening, you should clearly state your objective for the presentation. Audiences like to know what they're getting into. (They also like to make sure that they're in the right room.)

Don't make this section fancy, long, or complicated; just get right to it: "Today I'm going to present three strategies for developing high-performing virtual teams." You might even want to preview your three (or four or more) main points right away, as an overview for your audience. This serves as a roadmap for the presentation, letting the audience know what's coming when. If you display your main points on a slide, they will function as an agenda for your presentation that can be easily seen by both you and your audience.

This is also the section where you should confirm for your audience what they will take away from the presentation. As you craft the objective, consider what the audience wants and needs to hear about this topic and sell the benefits up front. For example: "Today I'm going to present three strategies for developing high-performing virtual teams. Once you understand these strategies, you will be able to turn your stressed, scattered, or siloed team members into a cohesive, productive, and satisfied team, no matter where everyone sits."

Main Points

How many main points can you include in a presentation? It simply depends on how long you have to speak. If you've got thirty minutes, you can probably include only a few aspects of your objective; if you've got three hours, you can include a lot more—or you can include more detail for each one.

This is where the sticky-note technique comes in handy. If you notice that you have more notes than will fit on your diamond, then you should take that as a warning that your presentation is getting much too complicated. Remember that your audience needs to remember what you say, and they can remember only so much at one sitting. As Henry David Thoreau would say, "Our life is frittered away by detail. Simplify, simplify."[10]

There are countless ways to organize your main points. Here are a few patterns to consider:

The Problem/Solution Framework

If your goal is to present a problem and offer a solution:

---

[10] Thoreau, Henry David. *Henry David Thoreau: Walden*. Cedar Lake, MI: ReadaClassic.com, 2010.

1. **Share the problem(s):** "We don't currently have a policy that dictates a fair distribution of sales commission when clients cross geographical areas."

2. **Share the impacts of the problem(s):** "The impacts include competition rather than collaboration between members of the sales team; reduced morale of employees; distrust of leadership; and unclear year-end performance-based bonuses."

3. **Offer one or more solutions:** "Salesperson A receives a higher percentage of the commission for cultivating the relationship and closing the sale; Salesperson B receives a lower percentage for 'owning' the geographical location of the client."

4. **Explain your reasoning for your recommendation(s):** "The solution needs to meet the overall needs of the company—to prioritize the acquisition of new clients—which is best done by supporting the salespeople responsible for client engagement, maintaining both salespeople's incentives, and setting a precedent for clear communication."

5. **Show how to implement your recommended solution(s):** "The sales force and leadership will work together to establish a formula for a fair distribution of commission to be used when clients cross geographical areas. Enlisting all players in the creation of the planning and writing of a clear policy, including the continued implementation moving forward, reinforces buy-in from all members of the team."

6. **Create a call to action:** "All employees continue to look at

ways they each use the company's goal, increasing the client base, to guide their behavior and actions in their individual roles within the company."

The Chronological Framework

If your goal is to help your audience understand a series of events, such as when you will launch a product, the history of your company, a progress report, or a crisis response plan, you can organize your main points by choosing a few relevant points in time using this framework:

- Twenty years ago
- Ten years ago
- Today

Or

- Today
- Five years from now
- In ten years

Or

- In Q1
- In Q2
- In this quarter

1. **Explain what happened at a specific point in time in the past.** "Last month, Monique and George sold software services to the XYZ Company. Monique cultivated the relationship and closed the sale, but XYZ Company is located in China (George's territory), not in India (Monique's territory)."

2. **Explain what is happening right now.** "Right now, Monique and George each believe they have earned the commission, and there is no clear, written policy in the company to guide the decision. This is currently creating a sense of competition rather than collaboration between members of the sales team."

3. **Explain what will happen at a specific point in the future.** "Beginning next quarter, the sales force and leadership will work together to establish a formula for a fair distribution of commission to be used when clients cross geographical areas."

The Geographic Framework

If you want to help your audience picture and understand different locations (geographically or spatially):

1. Explain what's happening globally.
2. Explain what's happening nationally.
3. Explain what's happening right here/locally.

Or

1. Explain what's happening nationally.
2. Explain what's happening in your region.
3. Explain what's happening in your city.

Or

1. Explain what happens in your factory.
2. Explain what happens in your distribution plant.
3. Explain what happens at corporate headquarters.

Pick a small representation of places or spaces that would comprise a compelling and informative presentation.

For example:

1. **Explain what's happening globally:** "In regions like Western Europe where marketing is regulated by the government, cigarette sales and rates of use are decreasing. Conversely, in areas where there is little regulation around the marketing of tobacco products, such as Asia and Africa, marketers are able to practice targeted advertising, which impacts the growing trend in sales and use."

2. **Explain what's happening nationally.** "In the United States, tobacco marketing remains heavily restricted. A downward trend in use for both adults and youth has been documented and directly correlates with increased regulation on marketing, including the prohibition of advertising on billboards, radio, and television. It can still be said that the largest predictor of tobacco use in the United States is socioeconomic status."

3. **Explain what's happening locally:** "Locally, tobacco education has been written into the state educational frameworks for pre-K through grade 12. Smoking is prohibited in restaurants and on school property and is frequently looked upon as a moral issue when parents discuss it with their children. It is a reality that children living in communities where the majority of the population is educated above the 12th grade, with a low percentage of working poor or disadvantaged, could grow up without

ever seeing an adult smoking. By taking smoking out of the range of 'normal' behavior, people are less likely to start and therefore do not become lifelong consumers of tobacco."

The Cause-and-Effect Framework

If your goal is to help your audience understand why something happened or is happening, or the effects of an action that was taken:

Decide whether you are going to share a *Single Cause with Many Effects*, a *Single Effect with Many Causes*, or *Multiple Causes and Effects*.

Single Cause with Many Effects

1. Explain the cause in detail.

2. Explain the primary effect and impact.

3. Explain the secondary effect and impact.

4. Explain additional contributing effects and impact.

Single Effect with Many Causes

1. Explain the effect in detail.

2. Explain the primary cause and impact.

3. Explain the secondary cause and impact.

4. Explain additional contributing causes and impact.

Multiple Causes and Effects

1. Explain cause 1, cause 2, and cause 3.

2. Explain effect 1, effect 2, and effect 3.

Or

1. Explain cause 1 and effect 1.

2. Explain cause 2 and effect 2.

3. Explain cause 3 and effect 3.

Example (Single cause with many effects):

1. **Explain the cause in detail:** "An unprecedented situation arose with the sales team that the current sales territory and commission structure does not address."

2. **Explain the primary effect and impact.** "Two different salespeople believe they deserve 100% of the commission, leading to conflict on the sales team."

3. **Explain the secondary effect and impact.** "The need to re-evaluate the sales territory and commission structure has led to a larger team of people coming together to collaborate and create a new policy."

The Middle-Ground Framework

If your goal is to help your audience find a moderate viewpoint, the middle ground, a win-win, or a compromise between two polarizing opinions or perspectives, or if your goal is to help a dissatisfied audience find temporary satisfaction:

1. **Acknowledge the audience's current perspective (no matter how polarizing it is) and explain the value of it.** This could also be the *current state*. "Currently, this small

family business meets only the minimum maternity leave required by law: eight weeks of unpaid leave. Women in the company have asked for twelve weeks of paid leave. Men in the company have remained silent. Women generally do not return to work after a maternity leave."

2. **Acknowledge the opposing point of view and explain how some people might have come to believe it to be true.** This could also be the *ideal state*. "Ideally, all employees would support a leave policy that encourages women and men to balance their personal lives with their employment. In this scenario, all employees would have adequate job protection in the event of pregnancy or adoption, and their benefits would match those offered to staff in larger businesses as a way of retaining employees post leave."

3. **Explain how the middle ground can offer a benefit to both sides, even if temporarily.** "Leadership in the company will come together with all employees to hear what is most valuable to them and make adjustments to their policy that both honor the time and/or compensation requested and the employers' own need for continuity of operations."

4. **Offer specifics regarding how the members of this audience can think about or take advantage of the middle ground as it relates to their current point of view.** "Businesses will see that when they support good employees to stay in their roles, increased costs toward those benefits will be an investment in building the entire organization and will not actually be perceived as financial losses."

Evidence Organization: The PREP Method

No matter how you structure your overall presentation, you will need some main points followed by support for those points. Use the **PREP** method to expand on your main points.

- **P: Name your point.** Your point should have a point of view attached to it. "Everyone should begin the day by eating a protein-rich breakfast" is more compelling than "Breakfast is the first meal of the day."

- **R: Explain your reason.** This is your justification for your point and point of view. "The reason that a protein-rich breakfast is so important is that it fills you up and keeps you fuller longer than if you just ate simple carbohydrates."

- **E: Share an example, evidence, or an experience that supports your point and reason.** "According to researchers at the University of Missouri, MRI scans of teenagers' brains showed that those who ate a high-protein breakfast experienced less brain activity in regions that control hunger than those who ate cereal for breakfast. The researchers concluded that a lower-protein breakfast doesn't keep people feeling full for as long as eating a higher-protein breakfast does."

Note: This section provides an excellent opportunity to bring your outside background and interests to your audience, including those of your native country or culture. You can make this section come alive for your audience by bringing in examples from outside of the immediate business or organizational context. Talk about how the news and current events relate to your topic. Draw from popular music, reference books, movies, television, or theater. Show how studies or research in other fields (medicine, engineering, psychology, economics, etc.) support your points. Share how other cultures and countries (including yours) deal with similar challenges or opportunities. As long as you keep a close connection between your example and the key point you're making, you can bring in other pieces of color and texture to illustrate your points in a creative and captivating way.

- **P: Your point, reiterated.** "And that's why I believe that everyone should begin the day by eating a protein-rich breakfast."

You can expand or contract the **PREP** framework according to whether you have multiple reasons for a specific point, or a single reason and multiple pieces of evidence, experience, or examples.

Evidence Organization: The Rule-of-Three Framework

If your goal is to bring together a range of ideas on a single topic in a structured, logical way that respects an audience's limited attention span:

1. **Explain your first main point, with supporting evidence.** "Emotional Intelligence (EQ) is a better predictor of success than IQ. In their book, *Emotional Intelligence 2.0*, authors Travis Bradbury and Jean Greaves note that studies across industry lines show that EQ predicts job performance 2-to-1 over any other skill."[11]

[11] Bradberry, Travis, Jean Greaves, and Patrick Lencioni. *Emotional Intelligence 2.0: The World's Most Popular Emotional Intelligence Test.* San Diego (California): TalentSmart, 2009.

2. **Explain your second main point, with supporting evidence.**
   "Unlike IQ, Emotional Intelligence can be improved. How? As Daniel Goleman, author of the best-selling book *Emotional Intelligence: Why It Can Matter More than IQ*, wrote, 'First you have to be motivated—ask yourself if you really care. Then you need a well-structured learning situation where, for instance, you have a clear picture of what you want to improve, and can practice specific behaviors that will help you enhance the targeted competence.'"[12]

3. **Explain your third main point, with supporting evidence.**
   "With the rapid growth of technology in the workplace—especially artificial intelligence—emotional intelligence is more important than ever. In their *Harvard Business Review* article, "The Rise of AI Makes Emotional Intelligence More Important," authors Megan Beck and Barry Libert note: 'Those that want to stay relevant in their professions will need to focus on skills and capabilities that artificial intelligence has trouble replicating—understanding, motivating, and interacting with human beings.'"[13]

Transitions

In order to make your main points come together fluently and fluidly, you need to connect and weave those points together through a logical flow of ideas. Transitions ease the listener into the next idea, provide internal structure, create suspense and intrigue, and serve to

[12] Goleman, Daniel. *Emotional Intelligence: Why It Can Matter More than IQ*. London: Bloomsbury, 2010.

[13] Beck, Megan and Barry Libert. "The Rise of AI Makes Emotional Intelligence More Important." *Harvard Business Review.* February 15, 2017. https://hbr.org/2017/02/the-rise-of-ai-makes-emotional-intelligence-more-important.

hold your whole presentation together. You need transitions between every section of your presentation so that your audience knows that the previous part has concluded and that a new section is coming. The better your transitions, the less work your listeners will have to do to keep track of what's happening. A disoriented audience is a disengaged audience.

Many of our clients (both native and nonnative English speakers) rely too heavily on using "also," "and," or "something else" as transitions. These get repetitive and boring. Here are some examples of better transitions you can use to help your main points come together:

- First and foremost . . .
- What else do we need to consider? We need to consider . . .
- The next point I'd like to address is . . .
- Let's take a look at . . .
- That brings us to . . .
- Also up for discussion is . . .
- In conclusion . . .
- Not only . . .
- First . . . second . . . third . . .
- Finally . . .
- With this in mind . . .
- What's more is that . . .
- Similarly . . .
- In contrast . . .
- Compare that with . . .

- Moreover . . .
- Surprisingly . . .
- Turning to . . .
- In the meantime . . .
- All things considered . . .

Recap

Here's a piece of simple advice often shared about how to make a presentation:

1. Tell them what you're going to tell them.

2. Tell them.

3. Tell them what you've told them.

The Recap is the part where you "tell them what you've told them." Quite simply, you'll remind the audience of the main points you just spoke about, before starting the Questions and Answers. It might seem silly to review what you just finished speaking about, but for an audience member who may have gotten temporarily distracted (or for anyone who might have had to leave the room for a few minutes), it's a useful tool to make sure everyone knows where you are. It's also a useful tool to make sure *you* remember where you are. And it also makes you sound organized and in control.

It doesn't have to be complicated. Here's an example:

"Before I take a few questions, let me quickly recap what I've covered so far. I shared with you where we opened new offices last year, then we discussed where we will be opening new offices over the next three to five years, and finally we discussed the implications for these expansions."

So simple, yet so necessary to keep everyone on track.

Questions and Answers (Q&A)

Assuming that your presentation includes a formal question-and-answer period, you will notice that the Presentation Diamond locates the Q&A *before* the conclusion and the closing. There are two important reasons for this placement:

1. **You want to be able to include any additional information in your conclusion that might have been raised during the Q&A.** If you do this, you will demonstrate to your audience that you were indeed listening to them. (This is particularly useful if the subject of your presentation is guaranteed to make a majority of audience members unhappy, like, "Why the Upcoming Budget Cuts are Mandatory" or something equally stressful.)

2. **What if the last question you get is one you can't answer?** What if the last thing the audience hears you say is, "I don't know. Oh, well, are there any other questions? No? Well, that's all I have, I guess . . ." That's not a very powerful closing.

When you formally conclude *after* the Q&A, your presentation will come across as much more polished and professional.

See chapter 12 for strategies on how to master the Q&A section of your presentation.

Conclusion

This section doesn't have to be complex or fancy. It can be a simple restatement of your objective, with a few observations thrown in that you collected during the Q&A. The point is to remind your audience of where they've been and what they've learned along the way. (This is also a useful technique if you're dealing with a hostile audience. The person who summarizes the discussion, no matter how heated or tense the discussion might have become, stays in control by having the last word.) Think of it as an opportunity to review the roadmap you set out in the Objective section—letting the audience know where you started, and where you are now—before you close the entire presentation.

Closing

Perhaps no section of a presentation is as important as the closing, since that's the last thing your audience will hear, and, therefore, the part of your message they will be most likely to remember from your entire presentation. Like openings, closings must never be just thrown away—they must be prepared and practiced.

Here are some famous last lines:

- ". . . that this government of the people, by the people, and for the people shall not perish from the earth." (Abraham Lincoln, *Gettysburg Address*)

- "Stay Hungry. Stay Foolish. And I have always wished that for myself. And now, as you graduate to begin anew, I wish that for you. Stay Hungry. Stay Foolish." (Steve Jobs, 2005 *Stanford Commencement Speech*)

- "I would draw a line half way between our poets and law-makers—between Dante and Blackstone—and place woman neither at man's feet nor above his head, but on an even platform by his side." (Elizabeth Cady Stanton, *Speech on the First Anniversary of the American Equal Rights Association*)

- "... free at last, free at last, great God Almighty, we are free at last." (Rev. Martin Luther King, Jr., *I Have a Dream Speech*)

Powerful stuff, yes? No wonder the closing is sometimes called the "climax."

Using a quote from a famous person to close a presentation is an excellent technique for adding a final dash of polish and pizzazz. Plus, it's the easiest thing to do, since all you have to do is find a suitable quote and plug it in. The only really tricky part is that you must memorize this final quote, as it looks unpolished and unprepared if you read it off a note card. (For this reason, we recommend that you stick to a short quotation.)

If you started with a statistic, you can end with one as well, or even revisit the original number from a new perspective. You can close with a short, concise, relevant story if you opened with one, or you can even offer the conclusion or epilogue to the same story you opened with. Doing so will give your presentation—and your audience—a sense of completion. You can even close with a rhetorical question. Who couldn't wrap it up that way? (That was an example of a rhetorical question—one that is used to make a point or for effect, rather than calling for a response.)

Chapter 4

Establish Rapport with Your Audience Despite Language and Cultural Barriers

You can make more friends in two months by becoming interested in other people than you can in two years by trying to get other people interested in you.

DALE CARNEGIE

An objective of any successful presentation is to build rapport with your audience. In other words, you want to deliver a presentation that is both engaging and inspiring; you do not want to lecture your audience as though they were students who don't have a clue as to what your topic is and should be addressed as if they were your intellectual inferiors.

In many business settings, audiences have come to expect that any presentation they attend will be both dry and uninteresting. Unfortunately, many presenters follow the school model, where the teacher does all the talking and the students silently take notes. This method may be efficient if all you want to do is transfer knowledge (just listen to a lecture on "The Influence of Baroque Architecture on

Papago Indian Dwellings," for example, take notes, and be prepared for a quiz on Monday). But if the objective of your presentation is to persuade your audience that your idea is both viable and useful, then you will need to involve them in your presentation. You will need to build *rapport* with them.

The word *rapport* (which comes from the French, *re-porter*, meaning "to bring back") is often defined as a sympathetic relationship or understanding. (In Chinese, rapport may be translated as 和 睦 关 系 *hémù guānxì*, which also means "tacit understanding." In Spanish, the term is *buena relación*, or "good relationship." In Filipino, it's *kaugnayan*, which has the sense of "affinity" and "connection.") When you establish rapport with your audience, you are setting up a dynamic of two-way communication in which the presenter and the audience members understand each other's point of view. The presenter sends out the message, and the audience responds to it, giving useful feedback to the presenter, who can then continue, make adjustments, or even stop based on that feedback.

It can seem to be an overwhelming problem if you are trying to establish rapport in a language that is not your native tongue. How can you build a connection with your audience if you are constantly trying to think of the correct word to use? Here are five tips for building rapport and engaging your audience no matter what language you speak.

1. **Do everything you can to learn about your audience.** The more you know about them, the easier it will be to identify what all you share in common. For example, if you know that the majority of folks in your presentation are just beginning

to learn about investing in the stock market, you can address their fears up front by sharing your own story of how you began your career as a stock analyst. Knowing your audience's level of expertise will also help you determine which terms to use and how many definitions and explanations you will need to provide.

It will also be helpful if you can gauge your audience's feelings about your topic before your presentation. Will most of them be open-minded and ready to accept new ideas from you? Or will they instead be closed-minded and set in their ways, so that you will need to make extra efforts to persuade them to consider your point of view?

Another factor to consider is the level of responsibility and authority among the attendees, especially if you are asking them to take some sort of action. Is the group made up of decision-makers? If so, then feel free to ask them to make a decision to buy your product, use your service, or approve your plan. However, if the people in your audience have neither the authority nor the responsibility to do what you're asking them to do, your presentation will be unsuccessful.

It can also be helpful to think about who else (other than you) may be asking your audience for their time, money, or other resources. If you're making a presentation to human resource professionals in which you're advocating for the promotion of two of your direct reports to director-level roles, acknowledge that your audience might be hearing multiple requests like this from your colleagues. If you're pitching your new software product to a group of IT professionals, recognize (out loud) that they are likely hearing pitches from your competitors as well. And while you don't want to say anything negative about other people (as it is likely to reflect poorly on you), you do want to demonstrate that you understand that your listeners may feel pulled in many directions. Have empathy for that and share how your recommendations, products, or services can make their decision-making easier.

Once you have a good idea about your audience's background, knowledge, and attitude, you can then address their concerns directly in your opening statements. As an example, one time Ellen was contracted to deliver a presentation on "The New Online Billing Service" to an audience of small-medical-practice administrators. From her research, she learned that most of them were very put off by the whole idea of this new way of doing things that they had been doing just fine for a long time. So, she began her presentation by asking them, "How many of you in this room do not see the need for a new computerized system?" Many hands were instantly raised. "How many of you think the old way of doing things was working just fine?" Again, many hands shot up. Then she said, "OK, I see where you are coming from. But what if I could show you that this new system would actually save you time and make your life a whole lot easier?" They were skeptical but intrigued. She had made a connection by acknowledging their point of view.

When Deborah was invited to present on "Coaching Skills for Human Resource Professionals," she realized that her audience would likely be a group of people who probably should know how to coach their colleagues, but might not want to admit that they didn't know how, or weren't doing it well. In order to help the audience reduce feelings of risk, vulnerability, or loss of credibility, Deborah shared: "I have been a certified professional coach with the International Coach Federation for more than a decade, and have coached hundreds of leaders across the globe, and yet I still learn something new about how to use coaching skills every single day. So, I'd like to thank you for giving me another opportunity to practice these skills, take some risks, make mistakes, and deepen my own learning—and I hope that many of you will take advantage of this opportunity, too."

One additional tip: If you are thrust into a presentation situation with little to no advance warning (the stuff of nightmares), you may need to survey your audience in the room in order to know more about what they already know about today's topic. You can do this simply and quickly with a poll, such as: "By a show of hands, how many of you have been working in this field for less than a year? How about up to three years? Four or more? A decade plus?" What you see in the room will give you an initial sense of how much background you might need to share. If you're feeling particularly bold, you might ask those with more experience to make themselves available for questions and concerns to those with fewer years of experience during the presentation. It will make more seasoned professionals feel recognized and valued, and it will take some of the pressure off of you.

2. **Ask questions to build instant rapport.** As shown in the example above, the simplest kind of question to ask is the survey question, in which you ask, "How many of you _____?" At the same time, you demonstrate what you want the audience to do by raising your own hand. (This gesture is common across cultures.) The question could be meant to learn more about your audience ("How many of you travelled more than two hours to get here today?") or to assess their feelings ("How many of you suffer from severe stage fright when you stand in front of an audience?") or to determine how open they are to your message ("How many of you believe in the old adage, 'If it isn't broken, don't fix it'?").

A riskier type of question to ask is the objective or test question, which requires a correct answer. ("Where is the Rock of Gibraltar?") If no one knows the answer, this kind of question will create an awkward pause. (And what will you do if someone does try to answer this question and their answer is wrong?) You should ask a test question at the beginning of your presentation only if you are relatively sure that no one in your audience will know the answer and if the answer is actually surprising. ("Who here knows how Nutella was invented?" Answer: Nutella was invented during World War II when an Italian pastry maker mixed hazelnuts into chocolate to extend his chocolate ration. Thank you, Italy!) ("Half of all humans who have ever lived have died from what?" Answer: malaria.) In general, you should either ask a question that most people will get right (creating a shared positive feeling of success) or ask a question that few people, if any, *would know* or *should know* (creating a shared feeling of challenge or suspense without singling anyone out).

3. **Begin with a personal story.** Storytelling is one of the oldest and most successful ways to connect with people from different backgrounds and cultures, including yours. When you begin your presentation with a personal story, you are inviting your audience to see the world through your eyes as you paint "word pictures" for them to see in their minds. "I'd like to begin today," you say, "by telling you about the time I _____." Suppose, for example, that you are making a presentation on cross-cultural communication, so you decide to begin by describing the time you were invited to dinner by your Chinese host and inadvertently sat in the seat that the host usually sits in. Or you explain your embarrassment at giving a gift to your Japanese host with your right hand or giving a gift to your Saudi Arabian host with your left hand. Make sure this story is relevant, relatable and short.

(For more evidence that starting with a story is a powerful presentation technique, watch the TED presentation by Sheena Iyengar[14] in which she begins by telling us the story of what happened when she asked for sugar with her tea in Japan.)

4. **Work on your accent—but don't obsess about it.** If English is your second language, you probably also have concerns that your foreign accent might make it difficult for your audience to understand you, leading them to become

[14] Iyengar, Sheena. "The Art of Choosing." Sheena Iyengar: The Art of Choosing | TED Talk | TED. com. July 2010. Accessed February 24, 2017. http://www.ted.com/talks/sheena_iyengar_on_the_art_ of_choosing?language=en.

disengaged. Nonnative English speakers usually carry over the intonation and phonetics of their native language, making their English sound foreign.

There are certainly many ways you can explore to modify your accent and adopt a neutral, General American or "newscaster accent" pronunciation.

The WikiHow site describes six of them:

- Learn about the International Phonetic Alphabet.
- Keep in mind that in English there is no matching association amid letters and sounds, as in different Romance languages.
- Practice.
- Participate in live shows.
- Sing.
- Search for a solid English-as-a-Second-Language (ESL) school and enroll.

Here are some additional suggestions that we've shared with our clients:

- Record your voice and isolate one or two pronunciation areas you'd like to improve—and practice those every day.
- Find an accent modification tutor.
- Record a few minutes of a TV show in which the characters speak in a neutral accent, and practice saying the lines along with them, mimicking the intonation and pronunciation.

While these suggestions are useful for nonnative English speakers, even native English speakers who present frequently might find these tips useful. Deborah, a third-generation native New Yorker (pronounced "New Yawkah" by natives of the region) has practiced using self-recording for several decades to sound "newscaster-neutral" while still being proud of her hometown. Check out this website to see how, even in America, accents have a wide range of pronunciations, intonations, and emphases: http://thechive.com/2013/06/06/american-accents-beautifully-mapped-22-hq-photos/.

If you don't have the time or inclination to follow these suggestions (after all, your accent is part of who you are and you shouldn't be embarrassed about it), then your next best bet is to help your audience understand you by using visuals, especially in the first few minutes of your presentation. Here is where a slide presentation program can be of tremendous help to you: Begin your presentation by showing the audience pictures of your main point(s). As the audience looks at the pictures, you can then narrate the meaning of each visual. Do not put a caption (or any other text) on the pictures you show. You want the audience to think about the picture as you speak, not read the text ahead of you.

You can even put up a picture and then ask the audience a question about it. In Ellen's presentation on how to avoid "Death by PowerPoint," she shows the audience a picture of a man who is fast asleep in the middle of an audience and asks them, "What is the caption for this picture?" This gets them engaged right away.

5. **Start off with an activity, exercise, or game.** This approach can be trickier than the simpler techniques for building rapport that we've discussed so far because it usually involves knowing and navigating your logistics: how many people will be in attendance? (You can't break them up into small groups if you have only a small group to begin with; if you have too many people, conducting an activity may be much too chaotic.) What kind of space will you be presenting in? (If the space is too small, there may not be enough room to move around comfortably; if the space is too large, it may be difficult to keep the audience focused.) Will you need props or physical materials to conduct the activity? How many will you need? What if you don't have enough? And most importantly, will you have enough time in your presentation to conduct the activity? (Facilitated exercises take up much more time than asking a couple of survey questions.)

Despite being complex, an activity, exercise, or game can be a powerful way for you to build rapport with your audience members and for your audience members to build rapport with one another. One of Ellen's favorite memories of a presentation that began with a facilitated exercise occurred during a trainer conference session on chaos theory. The presenter could certainly have begun the presentation by intoning (from Wikipedia): "Chaos theory is a field of study in mathematics which studies the behavior of dynamical systems that are highly sensitive to initial conditions—a response popularly referred to as the butterfly effect. Small differences in initial conditions (such as those due to rounding errors in numerical computation) yield widely diverging outcomes for such dynamical systems, rendering long-term prediction impossible in general. This happens even though these systems are deterministic, meaning that their future behavior is fully determined by their initial conditions, with no random elements involved. In other words, the deterministic nature of these systems does not make them predictable. This behavior is known as deterministic chaos, or simply chaos." (Snore. If we were sitting in the back row, we would sneak out now.)

Instead of starting with a definition of chaos theory, this presenter held up a large Nerf brand foam ball and said, "See this Nerf ball? I'm going to throw it into the audience [there were about fifty people in attendance] and whoever catches it must throw it to someone else, and so on and so on." As the audience watched the ball randomly move around the room chaotically, they became both engaged in and excited by the session's topic.

So, if you know how many people will be in your audience, what kind of space you will be presenting in, and what (and how many) materials you will need to conduct an activity, what kinds of exercises can you do? It all depends on what your topic and your objective is.

- **If you want to persuade your audience to buy your product:** Distribute samples to everyone and ask for feedback. Or distribute a sample to a group of participants and ask them to agree on their evaluation. Or ask for a volunteer (or several volunteers) to demonstrate how to use the product.

- **If you want to persuade your audience to buy your idea:** Distribute questionnaires before your presentation and then ask several members of the audience to share their responses. Or give one questionnaire to each group and ask them to agree on their responses.

- **If you want to update your audience on the status of a project:** Give individual audience members a questionnaire that asks them to describe the earlier status of the project and make predictions about where the project is now. Then tell them how close or far off their predictions are.

- **If you want to teach your audience about some area of knowledge (for example, "The Influence of Baroque Architecture on Papago Indian Dwellings"):** Play a version of the TV game show Jeopardy! with them by showing them pictures and asking them to identify what they see. (If you have time, you can even have them score their own answers, individually or in groups, to see who won the game.)

Deborah is a big fan of The Center for Creative Leadership's Visual Explorer, which offers a package of beautiful images printed on letter-sized paper, postcards, or playing cards used to facilitate creative conversations. It is simple enough to distribute the pictures to the audience members (or scatter them across the tables or on the floor) and ask people to choose one or more images that

- represent their current attitude to the topic of your presentation,

- look like how they want to feel about the topic of your presentation,

- highlight a concern or question they have about the topic,

- show the possibilities in the current situation,

- express the past or the future, or

- evoke what the organization would do with unlimited resources.

As you can imagine, the list is endless. And as you can also imagine, you can find some royalty-free pictures online to print out and use for this purpose. For more ideas for interactive games and activities to use in a presentation, visit http://www.thiagi.com/.

Whatever you do to build rapport with your audience, keep in mind the wisdom of poet and activist Maya Angelou: "I've learned that people will forget what you said, people will forget what you did, but people will never forget how you made them feel."

Chapter 5

Use Simple, Specific Language to Make a Memorable Impact

Dealing with complexity is an inefficient and unnecessary waste of time, attention, and mental energy. There is never any justification for things being complex when they could be simple.

PSYCHOLOGIST, PHYSICIAN, AND AUTHOR EDWARD DE BONO

O ne of the most common mistakes that presenters make is to try to impress their audience with their complex, sophisticated, and superior vocabulary. This seems to be especially true for nonnative speakers. "Notice how many polysyllabic words I am using," they seem to say. "Aren't you impressed by the breadth of my knowledge? Doesn't 'polysyllabic' sound much more impressive than 'having many syllables?' Look how fluent I am!" (Many native English speakers are guilty of this, too.)

There are two main problems with such an approach to public speaking: One, you run the risk of using such erudite words and terms incorrectly; two, if you use too many big words, you may puzzle your audience, not persuade them. (If you have to look up "erudite" in the dictionary, chances are your audience would have to as well. It means "characterized by great knowledge.")

The solution? Keep it simple. As Strunk and White wrote in their classic book, *The Elements of Style*, "Use definite, specific, concrete language."[16] Remember that your objective is to make a connection with your audience and to help them to understand and accept your point. If you use too many esoteric terms (ones that are intended for or likely to be understood by only a small number of people with a specialized knowledge or interest), you will likely disengage and even alienate your audience. As the American novelist, Mark Twain (who in his early days wrote for magazines and was paid by the word), once said, "I never write 'metropolis' for seven cents when I can get the same amount for 'city.'"

For those of you who make presentations on various business-related topics, the danger is to fall into the trap of using business jargon and buzzwords—words that sound important, but are so abstract that they convey little or no actual meaning. For examples, go to the *Wall Street Journal's* "Business Buzzwords Generator"[17] and you will find such lofty-sounding but meaningless statements as these:

- Our deep dive is the most out-of-the-box thing at our company. Do your best to gamify it.

- Next quarter we will launch our new low-hanging fruit-killer which will piggyback the learnings strategically.

- At the end of the day, it's time to act with passionate learnings and benchmark our team tipping point.

In a *Harvard Business Review* interview, "Business Jargon Is Not a Value-Add," Dan Pallotta, president of Advertising for Humanity

---

[16] Strunk, William, and E. B. (Elwyn Brooks) White. *The Elements of Style*. Macmillan Reference, 1962.
[17] "Business Buzzwords Generator - WSJ.com." *The Wall Street Journal*. Accessed February 24, 2017. http://projects.wsj.com/buzzwords2014/#p=7|31,4|32|0|||0.

and author of *Uncharitable*, said, "I think it's become a habit for us
. . . I think at a deeper level, people feel like they have to talk that way.
I think there are a lot of inferiority complexes. I think people have a
punishing voice in their heads that tells them they're dumb, and so
we try to mimic the things we hear other people say because we think
they're smarter than us. And it's not even so much coming from an
egotistical place. It's coming from just wanting to meet the threshold
of what's considered intelligent business vernacular."[18] ("Vernacular"
means "the native speech or language of a place; the language or
vocabulary peculiar to a class or profession." Ironic, right?)

If English is your second language, it makes sense that you may be
trying to "meet the threshold" of intelligent business conversation
in English. Nevertheless, your audience is not interested in whether
you could win an international spelling bee or successfully compete
on a trivia game show. They simply want to know what your point is
and why it is important to them.

Another trap that presenters fall into is using idioms that may or
may not have any real meaning for their audiences, depending on
their own cultural backgrounds. An idiom is a set expression or a
phrase comprising two or more words that are not intended to be
interpreted literally. For example, in English, we may refer to the
weather as "raining cats and dogs." We don't, of course, mean that
animals are literally falling out of the sky; we just mean that it's
raining really hard.

All cultures have their own idioms, which give a certain wonderful

---

[18]"Business Jargon Is Not a Value-Add." *Harvard Business Review*. March 30, 2015. Accessed February 24, 2017. https://hbr.org/2011/12/business-jargon-is-not-a-value.

poetry to their language, but often cannot be translated directly into another language. The Open Translation Project volunteers for TED Talks have found many such expressions[19]:

- **German:** *Tomaten auf den Augen haben*. Literal translation: "You have tomatoes on your eyes." Meaning: "You are not seeing what everyone else can see."

- **Swedish:** *Det är ingen ko på isen*. Literal translation: "There's no cow on the ice." Meaning: "There's no need to worry."

- **French:** *Les carottes sont cuites!* Literal translation: "The carrots are cooked!" Meaning: "The situation can't be changed."

- **Russian:** Хоть кол на голове теши. Literal translation: "You can sharpen an ax on top of his head." Meaning: "He's a very stubborn person."

- **Japanese:** 猫をかぶる. Literal translation: "To wear a cat on one's head." Meaning: "You're hiding your claws and pretending to be a nice, harmless person."

- **Chinese:** 半途而废 (bàn tú ér fèi). Literal translation: "To walk half the road and give up." Meaning: "To give up halfway."

We are not suggesting that you never use idioms of any kind in your presentations; we are merely suggesting that you be sure to check with your audience for their understanding. For example, once while teaching a business communications class in Beijing, Ellen wanted to stress that the first students to arrive at class on the following day

---

[19] "40 Brilliant Idioms That Simply Can't Be Translated Literally." TED Blog. August 10, 2015. Accessed February 24, 2017. http://blog.ted.com/40-idioms-that-cant-be-translated-literally/.

would have first choice of speaking times. So, she asked her students, "Does everyone here understand the expression, 'The early bird gets the worm'?" With a little help from the more fluent English speakers in the class, they quickly grasped her meaning.

You can use this technique in your presentations as well. For example, if you are Chinese and you want to explain the concept of rapport to your English-speaking audience, you might say, "In English, you all know what the French word rapport means, yes? Well, in Chinese, we may say *hémù guānxì* (和 睦 关 系), which has a similar meaning." (You might even put the characters for this phrase up on your slide and explain that 和 means harmony, peace; 睦 means amiable or peaceful; and 关 系 means a close connection.) As long as you explain the idiom you are using, your audience will be able to understand you.

Besides the use of obscure idioms, an additional challenge for nonnative speakers is recognizing when a word, phrase, or even an acronym has a negative meaning in English that doesn't seem immediately evident in your native tongue. When Deborah worked with a group of French-, Spanish-, and Chinese-speaking business leaders on a new entrepreneurial endeavor that they were pitching, she was taken aback to see how proudly they rattled off their consulting firm's acronym:

Strategic
Communications
And
Management
Solutions

Why was this a problem? Because in English "scam" is defined as (noun) "confidence games or other fraudulent schemes, especially for making a quick profit; swindle; and (verb) to cheat or defraud." It's definitely not a company name that inspires confidence!

Make sure that you check the more subtle meanings of words, phrases, and acronyms with a native English speaker before you share them widely and publicly.

One even more dangerous tactic for somebody speaking to a Western audience is to insert a joke in the presentation. Even if you are adept at telling jokes to your friends or family in informal situations, there is no guarantee that you will have the same success with a group of strangers, particularly if they come from a different cultural background. The humor in most jokes works because of a shared frame of reference; if you and your audience members do not share the same cultural worldview, you risk confusing them (at the least) or alienating them (at the worst). When Ellen's Chinese students asked her once if it would be a good idea to tell a joke in a presentation, she told them a distinctly American joke: "Two cannibals are having dinner. One cannibal turns to the other and says, 'I hate my mother-in-law.' The other cannibal says, 'Well, just eat the noodles.'" Do you think that was funny? If you are native-born American, if you understand the stereotype of how Americans feel about their mothers-in-law, and if you know what a cannibal is, then you might find this joke amusing (or at least you will get it). If you don't have this cultural knowledge, you may be puzzled, or even concerned (as, indeed, Ellen's Chinese students were).

The worst-case scenario is that the joke you tell will be offensive to members of your audience. (Certainly, those members who actually love and honor their mothers-in-law might be insulted. Both Ellen and Deborah would like to note, for the record, that they love and honor theirs.) If you tell a joke at the beginning of a presentation and it has a negative impact on your audience, the rest may well be a disaster. It's not worth the risk to even try this form of humor.

The best way to add humor to your presentation is to tell a personal story. If the target of your humor is yourself, you will most likely offend no one, and—even better—you will establish a human connection between yourself and your audience, no matter how different your cultural frames of reference may be.

One important tip about adding humor: don't tell your audience that you're about to tell them a funny story—just tell it. If they laugh, great. If they don't, then it was just a story, which is fine, too. You don't want to set yourself up for embarrassment if your story doesn't have exactly the impact you hoped for.

What's the bottom line? Keep your language simple, clear, and free from possible misinterpretations and misunderstandings. As business leader Lee Iacocca once said, "You can have brilliant ideas, but if you can't get them across, your ideas won't get you anywhere."

Chapter 6

Use Gestures, Movement, and Facial Expressions to Engage Your Audience

Love the moment and the energy of that moment will spread beyond all boundaries.

ARTIST CORITA KENT

In their *Harvard Business Review* article, "Connect, Then Lead," authors Amy Cuddy, Matthew Kohut, and John Neffinger share the following research results, which we briefly mentioned in Chapter 2: "When we judge others—especially our leaders—we look first at two characteristics: how lovable they are (their warmth, communion, or trustworthiness) and how fearsome they are (their strength, agency, or competence). Although there is some disagreement about the proper labels for the traits, researchers agree that they are the two primary dimensions of social judgment."[20]

When you are making a presentation, you are facing—and trying to positively influence—social judgment. These two elements, warmth and strength, are held in high regard (and are in high demand) for leaders in Western cultures. And as the authors also note, "We

---

[20] Cuddy, Amy, Matthew Kohut, and John Neffinger. "Connect, Then Lead." *Harvard Business Review.* November 02, 2014. https://hbr.org/2013/07/connect-then-lead.

notice plenty of other traits in people, but they're nowhere near as influential as warmth and strength. Indeed, insights from the field of psychology show that these two dimensions account for more than 90 percent of the variance in the positive or negative impressions we form of the people around us."[21]

Every presentation is an opportunity to create a positive impression. And while the verbal language you use, as well as your tone of voice, can signal to your audience how to feel and think about you, no element of communication is more powerful and influential than your body language.

First, let's define body language. It's the visual message you send without speaking, transmitted simply by the way your body moves in space. For example, if I think your idea is a bad one and will never work, I don't have to actually say so. I can just shake my head from side to side (meaning "no"), frown, and cross my arms. No matter what language you speak, you will get the point.

[21] Ibid.

Some body language, however, has a particular meaning for different cultures. Consider this particular hand gesture:

In the United States, this hand position typically means "okay" and is usually a very positive gesture. ("How is the project going?" "Okay!") In the Mediterranean region, however, and in Russia, Brazil, and Turkey, this gesture may be perceived as a sexual insult. In Tunisia, France, and Belgium, it indicates zero (or worthless). ("How is the project going?" "It's worthless!")

This sign, in American usage, typically means victory or peace, two very positive concepts. In Australia, New Zealand, and Malta, however, it can mean "Up yours!" (Not a very nice message at all.)

And then there's this hand gesture, which means "Everything is going great" in America, but can mean "Sit on this!" in Australia.

These potentially offensive gestures are not used all that often, and you will probably be all right if you just make a mental note to avoid them. The major problem with body language, when presenting to a Western audience, is the lack of it: A presenter who uses essentially no body language will not be considered persuasive or appealing. If you hide behind a lectern, sweaty palms gripping the sides, your head down as you read your notes (or your head swiveled backwards as you read your slides), your audience is most likely going to fall asleep, start texting, begin reading e-mail, or slip out of the room altogether.

As a presenter, you want to be aware of your own cultural norms around nonverbal communication, as well as the cultural norms and expectations of the audience to whom you're presenting. In her article, "How Historical Migration Patterns Shape Emotional Expression" (for the *Society for Personality and Social Psychology Character & Context Blog*), Adrienne Wood shares that, in countries where immigration rates are historically high, people are more likely to find common language in facial expressions and body language "in order to compensate for lack of common norms and language." In heterogeneous cultures, people are more likely to have greater emotional expressivity (facial expressions, body language, and other nonverbal components) in order to make themselves understood through communication channels other than verbal speech, and this expressivity is passed down through generations. In contrast, "cultures whose populations have stayed put for hundreds of years and are therefore relatively more homogeneous, such as Japan and Norway, have shared cultural knowledge, norms, and language, and so can rely on more than clear, big expressions of emotion."[22]

[22] Wood, Aderienne. "Character & Context." How Historical Migration Patterns Shape Emotional Expression | SPSP. http://spsp.org/blog/how-historical-migration-patterns-shape-emotional-expression.

Based on Wood's research, you can expect Americans, Canadians, and Australians to be among the most emotionally expressive, and Chinese, Japanese, North Africans, and Scandinavians to be less so. (You can see the map at the website listed in the footnote on page 70.) It's helpful to think about your own preferences and norms, and then have a plan for adapting to those of your audience.

When it comes to making a presentation to an English-speaking audience, the following three techniques can help you get your point across dynamically, persuasively, and in an appropriately expressive manner:

1. **Be sure to make deliberate eye contact with as many audience members as you can.** This technique involves turning your head from side to side and up and down as you briefly (for a few seconds) look at each person in turn. If you stare at the ceiling, or the back of the room, or your notes, or your slides, your audience will find you to be untrustworthy. (American audiences, in particular, determine a person's trustworthiness by how steadily they make eye contact. A person who does not "look you in the eye" is not to be trusted.)

   This technique may be more difficult for some speakers, especially those brought up in a culture that considers assertive eye contact to be rude. (Women may be particularly handicapped by this cultural norm.) In her *New York Times* article, "Psst. Look Over Here," writer Kate Murphy cites research showing that it "varies by culture how long before mutual gazers break eye contact. For example, the Japanese tend to avert their eyes more quickly than those in Western cultures." She also cites a study conducted by Japanese and Finnish researchers that

71

found that "Japanese subjects tended to perceive another's face as being more angry, unapproachable, and unpleasant when making eye contact compared with individuals from a Western European culture."[23]

That being said, you want to make eye contact that is briefly but meaningfully sustained rather than having a stare-down. While eye contact that is too fleeting can make you seem nervous, eye contact that is too intense signals intimacy or combat—neither of which is appropriate for any business presentation. What does "meaningful" mean? Sustained for three to five seconds, without dodging back and forth between people, or staring for so long that it becomes uncomfortable.

You can overcome your own cultural norms and/or fear of eye contact by practicing in front of a live audience and receiving feedback from them as to how often you look at them. (Having yourself videotaped will also help you improve.)

If you're willing to work with a test audience before a big presentation, you can use the exercise that Deborah and Ellen lead in their workshops to help participants practice making eye contact while speaking in public: Prepare a three- to five-minute presentation to deliver to a group of five to ten people. Ask each member of the group to keep his or her hand raised until you have made meaningful eye contact with them three times. They can then lower their hands. When everyone has put his or her hand down, you're done—and you will have practiced visually connecting with everyone more than once.

[23] Murphy, Kate. "Psst. Look Over Here." *The New York Times*. May 16, 2014. https://www.nytimes.com/2014/05/17/sunday-review/the-eyes-have-it.html.

2. **Smile to show that you're happy to be there.** Few ways of communicating are more culturally influenced than smiling; thus, unless you're delivering disappointing or devastating news, you should smile (at least a little bit) when presenting to American audiences. Your smile is an important way of signaling to the audience that you are honored to have this opportunity to speak with them and that you're happy to do so. And yes, you should do it even if you're not feeling particularly honored or happy to be making a presentation!

While in other parts of the world smiling may be much less common, in the United States, it signals confidence, openness, and an invitation to build rapport. You might be surprised (and pleased) to find that when you smile, people smile in return. We understand that this may feel unnatural or insincere to you—and we also understand that not smiling can lead to misunderstandings, hurt feelings, and even the perception that you're being disrespectful.

In the words of Vietnamese Buddhist monk, teacher, and peace activist Thich Nhat Hanh, "Sometimes your joy is the source of your smile, but sometimes your smile can be the source of your joy."

3. **Come out from behind the lectern when possible.** If you need a microphone because the room is large and your audience members are many, ask for a lavalier mic or a "diva mic" (the kind that peeks out from behind your ear), so you can wear it and move around hands-free. The podium or lectern will create a barrier between you and your audience,

suggesting that you do not actually want to make contact—you just want to get the ordeal over as quickly as possible. (And even if that is the case, you don't want your audience to know it). On the contrary, if you approach your audience during your talk, you will strengthen the connection between them and you. Just be sure that wherever you stand, you do not block the slides from anyone in the audience.

When you stand behind the lectern, or sit behind a table, or preside over a dais, you are establishing your territory as separate from the space your audience inhabits. When you move into their space, you establish a sense of togetherness with your listeners.

Your main objective should always be to move where you can see all of your listeners and they can see you easily. It's much easier to understand people—and easier for them to understand you—if you can actually watch their mouths moving. Do not let the furniture dictate where you will stand.

4. **Learn to make effective hand gestures.** While you're moving around the presentation space, manipulating the dynamics with your entire body, what are you supposed to be doing with your hands? Are they locked in front of you or behind? Are they stuffed into your pockets? Are they playing with a pointer, or a marker, or a slide controller? Are they toying with your necktie or your necklace? Are they twiddling your mustache? Spinning your wedding ring? Or are they doing what they're supposed to—illustrating your main points with punctuation and emphasis?

Excellent presenters use gestures that add to, rather than distract from, the presentation. "Suit the action to the word, the word to the action," said Shakespeare's Hamlet to the players. Easy for Hamlet to say, since he wasn't standing in front of a skeptical group of first-level line managers about to endure an eight-hour seminar entitled, "A Total Quality Approach to Valuing Diversity and Managing Change while Thriving on Chaos." How do you know which gestures are suitable, which facial expressions appropriate?

In general, Western (English-speaking) audiences prefer a speaker who moves and gestures dynamically and, at times, dramatically, using his or her hands to punctuate the main points of the presentation.

One of the simplest, most audience-friendly gestures to adopt for Western-style presentations is open, uplifted palms that gesture out toward your listeners. According to the Center for Nonverbal Studies, "uplifted palms suggest a vulnerable or nonaggressive pose that appeals to listeners as allies rather than as rivals or foes. Throughout the world, palm-up cues reflect moods of congeniality, humility, and uncertainty."[24] In contrast, palm-down gestures come across as more domineering and aggressive. Therefore, if you're going to use palm-down gestures, use them sparingly. Think of palm-up gestures as the main dish, and palm-down gestures as the spice. Too little spice and the meal has no flavor. Too much, and it's inedible. Of course, you always have the option to put

---

[24]"Palm Up." Center for Nonverbal Studies. Accessed March 08, 2017. http://center-for-nonverbal-studies.org/htdocs/palmup.htm.

your hands down by your sides and rest between gestures. This gives you a rest, and your audience's eyes a rest, too. Nevertheless, a presenter who hides behind the lectern, or stands still as a stone, or clenches his hands, or wags his finger, or crosses her arms will be perceived by the audience as one who is not sincere, not persuasive, or not professional. Here are some body language positions to use regularly, as well as some to use sparingly.

Use regularly:

"Everyone is welcome here."   "Here's what's in it for you."

"Isn't it wonderful!"

"This affects me, too."

"My third point is . . ."

"Pay attention because
this is important."
(highlighting a point)

Use Sparingly:

"Go ahead, make me
believe you."

"Not sure that I
agree with you."

"Let me think about that for
a while. I'm not sure."

"Guess what's in my pockets."

How to Stand:

Balanced, feet shoulder
width apart, arms relaxed.

Use sparingly:

Crossed legs, leaning to one side.

You can't choreograph your gestures without coming across as awkward or fake; your best strategy is to watch other presenters and learn from them how to move and gesture effectively. Here are some presenters to watch:

- In her video, "Your Body Language Shapes Who You Are," social psychologist Amy Cuddy explains how to use "power poses" to make yourself appear more confident and assured (which, in turn, will make you feel more confident and assured).[25]

- Steve Jobs was a master presenter who knew how to use effective body language to both engage his audience and persuade them to buy Apple's newest product. You can watch Jobs presenting at the unveiling of the iMac G4 and notice how he uses animated gestures and facial expressions and moves around on the stage purposefully.[26]

- Also take a look at the video of Scott Harrison, the founder and CEO of Charity-Water, and pay particular attention to his movement and gestures.[27]

- And lastly, check out the video by Dananjaya Hettiarachchi, from Sri Lanka, who became the World Champion of Public Speaking in 2014.[28]

[25]Cuddy, Amy. "Your Body Language Shapes Who You Are." Amy Cuddy: Your Body Language Shapes Who You Are | TED Talk | TED.com. June 2012. https://www.ted.com/talks/amy_cuddy_your_body_language_shapes_who_you_are.

[26]"IMac G4 Unveiling." YouTube. January 7, 2002. https://www.youtube.com/watch?t=24&v=YxRcQfALqqw.

[27]Scott Harrison, Founder & CEO, Charity-Water Shares His Story at LeWeb Paris 2012. Produced by Leweb.co. Performed by Scott Harrison. Vimeo. Accessed February 26, 2017. https://vimeo.com/112727142.

[28]Hettiarachchi, Dananjaya. "Dananjaya Hettiarachchi World Champion of Public Speaking 2014 - Full Speech." YouTube. September 22, 2014. https://youtu.be/bbz2boNSeL0.

Find as many examples as you can of powerful public speakers and learn from them. "We all receive a weird education," said the French classical actor Jean-Louis Barrault. "We are taught how to write. We are taught, to a lesser degree, how to speak. But we rarely if ever are taught how to move."[29]

It's never too late to learn.

[29]Jean-Louis, Barrault. "Child of Silence." Translated by Eric Bentley. In *Theatre Arts on Acting*, edited by Laurence Senelick. London: Routledge, 2008.

Chapter 7

Speak Up to Be Heard

Stand before the people you fear and speak your mind—even if your voice shakes.

AMERICAN SOCIAL ACTIVIST AND FOUNDER OF THE
GRAY PANTHERS, MAGGIE KUHN

n chapter 2, we discussed the importance of speaking more slowly, especially if you have an accent or tend to speak very quickly, and we also talked about the power of the dramatic pause. Now let's consider some other aspects of your public speaking voice, particularly volume, pitch, and pace.

If your audience cannot hear you easily, it doesn't matter what your accent is. So how do you know if they can hear you? Well, you could ask them, "Can everyone hear me?" Pay particular attention to the people in the back of the room as you ask this question. If everyone nods yes, then you're good to go. But what if they tell you they can't hear you? What should you do?

You should *project your voice* so that it resonates in the space.

Projecting your voice is not the same as shouting at your audience. Indeed, if you shout at them, they will probably get up and leave.

Projection is a technique that stage actors have used for hundreds and hundreds of years (before there were microphones) to ensure that every audience member in the "house" (whether it be a small theater or a large amphitheater) can hear them clearly.

You can discover what your own voice sounds like when you project rather than shout, but first, you need to record yourself speaking. With the recorder on, try shouting. Shout out anything—your name, a quote, a nonsense phrase, whatever. Play this back and listen to yourself. Do you sound strident? (Synonyms for "strident" are harsh, raucous, rough, grating, rasping, jarring, loud, shrill, screeching, piercing, and ear-piercing.) Does your voice sound forced or too high-pitched?

Next, do this: Put your hands on your diaphragm, which is located under your lungs. (The diaphragm is a dome-shaped, muscular partition separating the thorax from the abdomen in mammals. It plays a major role in breathing, as its contraction increases the volume of the thorax, and so inflates the lungs.) Now whisper the same phrase you shouted earlier. Whisper as loudly as you can, and feel what happens to your diaphragm as you do so. Did you feel it tighten?

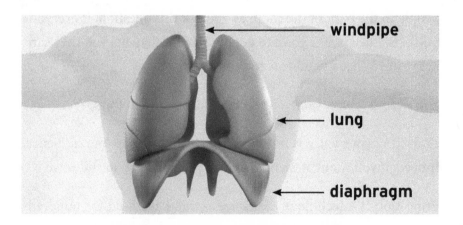

Now tighten (contract) your diaphragm without saying anything. Keep your hands there so you can feel your diaphragm tighten. Relax. Tighten again. Relax. Now consciously tighten your diaphragm and speak the same phrase you shouted earlier. Play back and listen to your voice. Does it sound louder? Stronger? More resonant?

If you practice consciously tightening your diaphragm when speaking, you will notice a gradual improvement in your vocal projection abilities. It won't happen overnight, but it will happen eventually if you practice. Remember, actors go through years of vocal training to develop their voices. By the way, this exercise will also help you to overcome any "breathy" qualities in your voice.

Here is another exercise you can do by yourself to improve your vocal projection. As you drive in your car, turn on some music. Consciously tighten your diaphragm and sing along with your favorite songs. Don't just hum. Don't just mouth the words. Sing! Belt it out! It doesn't matter if you can't sing on-key or well. You're in your car. Who's going to hear you? Practice this exercise regularly, and you'll eventually hear the difference as your speaking voice changes to a lower, more resonant register.

Now let's consider the problem of pitch—specifically a voice that is too high-pitched. (The opposite, a low-pitched voice, is rarely a problem.) Pitch refers to the quality of a sound governed by the rate of vibrations producing it or the degree of highness or lowness of a tone. According to author, legal consultant, and communication coach David Parnell, evolutionary psychology suggests that people of both sexes respond better to deep male voices than high female voices. While it is true that more women than men have high-pitched voices, there are some men who have naturally high tenor voices. A well-known example of an actor with a tenor voice was Laurence Olivier, who famously played the part of Othello in 1965 wearing black makeup (very controversial) and who worked diligently before the performance to lower the register of his naturally high-pitched voice from that of a tenor to a basso-profundo.

In her book, *The Human Voice*[30], journalist, sociologist, and radio broadcaster Anne Karpf cites some fascinating cultural differences regarding pitch:

- Women in almost every culture speak in deeper voices than Japanese women.

- American women's voices are lower than Japanese women's.

- Swedish women's voices are lower than American women's voices.

- Dutch women's voices are lower than Swedish women's voices.

Karpf notes that vocal difference is one way of expressing social difference, and cites studies claiming that as soon as words are uttered, it's possible to determine the speaker's biological, psychological, and social status, as well as select physical (size, height, sex, age) and social (occupation, sexual orientation) information. For Dutch speakers, for example, whose native society doesn't significantly differentiate between its image of the ideal male and the ideal female, there are few differences between the male and female voice.

Learning how to control your diaphragm, as we discussed above,

[30]Karpf, Anne. *The Human Voice: How This Extraordinary Instrument Reveals Essential Clues about Who We Are.* London: Bloomsbury Pub. Plc., 2006.

will help you speak with more resonance and thus lower your pitch.

Lastly, let's discuss the concept of pace, which is the speed at which you speak. Basically, there are two items to consider when adjusting the pace of your speaking voice:

1. Speak at the right pace, neither too fast nor too slow.

2. Vary your pace so that you do not speak in a monotone.

What is the right pace? According to the National Center for Voice and Speech, the average rate for English speakers in the United States is about 150 words per minute. To test this for yourself, set a timer for one minute and then read the following passage (from *A Tale of Two Cities* by Charles Dickens) out loud:

> *It was the best of times, it was the worst of times, it was the age of wisdom, it was the age of foolishness, it was the epoch of belief, it was the epoch of incredulity, it was the season of Light, it was the season of Darkness, it was the spring of hope, it was the winter of despair.*
>
> *We had everything before us, we had nothing before us, we were all going direct to Heaven, we were all going direct the other way—in short, the period was so far like the present period, that some of its noisiest authorities insisted on its being received, for good or for evil, in the superlative degree of comparison only.*
>
> *There were a king with a large jaw and a queen with a plain face, on the throne of England; there were a king with a large jaw and a queen with a fair face, on the throne of France.*

(159 words)

How did you do? Did you finish the passage within one minute, ending close to sixty seconds? If you did, then you have a normal speaking pace. If you finished with many seconds left over, you speak too quickly; if you finished with words still left to speak and no more seconds, then you speak too slowly. See if you can practice the pace of this passage until you end up right around sixty seconds.

When you've got a normal Western speaking pace down, next try to see if you can vary the pace when speaking the same passage out loud. Pick certain sentences to speak quickly.

For example, you could increase the speed of your pace when saying, *"We had everything before us, we had nothing before us, we were all going direct to Heaven, we were all going direct the other way."* Speaking more quickly here would reinforce the concept that we were all moving very quickly, no matter what the direction.

Then try speaking the next sentence more slowly: *"In short, the period was so far like the present period, that some of its noisiest authorities insisted on its being received, for good or for evil, in the superlative degree of comparison only."* Speaking more slowly here would create a sense of gravitas, seriousness, and importance.

Such variety in your pace will make your delivery much more interesting for your listeners, and they will pay more attention to your main points. As Mahatma Gandhi said, "There is more to life than increasing its speed." There is more to making a speech than increasing its speed, too.

Chapter 8

Partner with Your Audience

We're all working together. That's the secret.

BUSINESSMAN SAM WALTON

Too many presenters think of a presentation as a lecture, in which a professor does all the talking and the students simply take notes. While this style may work in college (where the audience wants to please the instructor to get good grades), it is not nearly as effective in the world of business, where the objective is to persuade your audience to accept your key points. An engaging presentation is different from a lecture.

As Lisa Braithwaite (author of the blog "Speak Schmeak") puts it: "A lecture is a one-way spiel that doesn't invite audience interaction, assumes the speaker is the keeper of all the knowledge, and puts the speaker above the listeners."[31]

A *presentation*, on the other hand (as we are using the term in this book), has a much more fluid structure and involves frequent audience participation. The presenter, for example, may periodically ask the audience a question or show a visual aid (a picture, a model, a simulation, etc.) to spur the audience's interest and involve them

---

[31]Braithwaite, Lisa. "Lecture versus Presentation." Speak Schmeak. September 9, 2011. http://www.speakschmeak.com/2011/09/lecture-vs-presentation.html.

in the presentation, making them active participants rather than passive receivers of information. One way to think about this is to imagine reading a classic children's book to a group of youngsters. You could simply read the book out loud while the children listen passively (lecture mode). Or you could pause periodically to ask a question ("What do you think happened next to the prince?") or show the children pictures from the book (presentation mode).

Ellen's mother was a librarian, and her favorite job was reading children's books to children of all ages. She was adept at getting her audience involved in the performance. She would stop in the middle of a suspenseful tale, put the book down, and then say to the audience: "I can't go on! It's too scary!"

And of course, the kids would yell back at her, "Keep reading! Keep reading!" until she gave in and continued with the story (having captured their complete attention). What works to keep children involved would also surely work to keep busy and distracted adults involved.

Here are seven ways to involve the audience in your presentation:

1. **Ask questions.** As we discussed in chapter 3, there are basically three types of questions: the survey question ("How many people here have been to China?"), the test question ("Where is the Rock of Gibraltar?"), and the how-do-you-feel question ("What is the biggest problem facing our company today?").

   No matter which type of question you decide to ask, resist the urge to answer it yourself. For example, instead of asking, "So how do you think this new process will affect our company's bottom line?" and immediately answering, "It will be very effective" just ask, "So how do you think this new process will affect our company's bottom line?" and then wait for a response. Just keep in mind that you will need to be prepared to handle whatever answers emerge. And if you know that you don't want to risk hearing a particular answer—especially in front of a group or a senior leader—*don't ask the question.*

You also have the option of asking the audience to break into pairs or small groups to discuss a question you have posed to the whole group. Remember that if you're the type of person who feels more comfortable speaking in front of smaller rather than larger groups, many of your audience members may feel the same way. A pair or triad is much more comfortable for many people than answering a question in front of the whole room.

2. **Use a Parking Lot.** If your audience has questions for you, it means they're listening and engaged (even if questions are the last thing you want from them). But sometimes, the audience has more questions than you can handle in the moment, or even in the overall amount of time you have scheduled to present. If you notice this happening, set up a "Parking Lot"—a simple piece of flipchart paper or a white board where you can write down questions that you will address later. You can write down the questions as they arise, or you can hand over a marker (or give out sticky notes) and ask the questioner to write down his or her question on the board. In addition to helping you keep track of questions,

it also gets the audience involved in the presentation by actively contributing—and having a visual representation of their contributions.

Deborah notes that in her presentations, she often sets up two Parking Lots: Short-Term Parking for those questions that she will be able to address during or immediately after the presentation, and Long-Term Parking for those questions that she will need to address individually with participants after the conclusion of the meeting. Note that if you're going to set up parking lots, your participants will expect you to address what you've parked there. It builds trust, credibility, and rapport to honor your commitment, even if you have to respond via phone or e-mail a day or two after the presentation.

3. **Check for understanding frequently.** Another way to keep your audience involved is to confirm that your audience is following you, simply by asking things like, "You see?" or "Is that clear to everyone?" and then waiting for feedback. If you are actually *not* being clear, this creates the perfect opportunity to learn from your audience and then try to make your point in a different way (one that might be more understandable). Pausing to check on your audience's comprehension is also very valuable if your accent may indeed be difficult for them to understand.

   A more advanced technique is to ask the audience, "What can I clarify for you?" This gives the audience a feeling of permission to ask you for additional information or to repeat something they didn't quite get the first time, and it makes you appear confident enough to ask for feedback mid-presentation. You might also pause to ask, "Of everything we've covered so far, what was most interesting/surprising/helpful?" It's another way to get information about what's working well for this audience, and what might not be resonating or completely clear.

4. **Create a Quiz or Game.** Who says a presentation needs to be boring? Give your audience a pop quiz by asking them some questions about your content halfway through the presentation. Make sure it's easy enough that participants will feel successful, but not so easy that you insult their intelligence. You can say something like, "Before we move to the second half of the presentation, let's do a quick check in to make sure we're on track. Okay, question one: What were our sales for Q3? Below average, average, or above average? Let's see a show of hands for who thinks sales were below average. . . ." This gets people involved, and it also reminds them to pay attention, in case they thought they could drift off during your presentation.

You can also create a game (perhaps by following the popular Jeopardy! format). Make it simple and fun. Imagine, for example, that you let people know there will be a Jeopardy!-type game before the end of the presentation; then they will really have to listen and remember what you shared with them. Toward the end, you can set up a few categories (such as "Countries We Began Exporting To this Year" or "New Hires this Quarter") and then pose some answers, calling on the audience for the questions.

For "Countries We Began Exporting To this Year," you might offer:

Answer: This European country produces 43 percent of the world's olive oil, shares a border with France, and its national anthem has no words. (**Question:** What is Spain?)

Or, for "New Hires this Quarter," you might offer:

Answer: This new employee graduated from the University of Florida, was a former police officer, and drinks three Diet Cokes before lunch. (**Question:** Who is Sharon Davidson?)

5. **Have the group do some work.** Humorist Dave Barry once said, "If you had to identify, in one word, the reason why the human race has not achieved, and never will achieve, its full potential, that word would be 'meetings.'"

   Part of the reason why people dread meetings is because they are often all lectures about work that has been done and that still needs to be done—they rarely involve doing actual work. One way to engage your listeners is to have them do some actual work in the meeting: Have them identify customer objections, or brainstorm new product offerings, or come up with a new name for an old initiative.

6. **Ask for a volunteer.** Want a simple solution to get your listeners involved? Ask for a volunteer to read a PowerPoint slide aloud, another one to hand out materials, and a different one to take notes on a flip chart or collect items from the audience.

7. **Use your slides as an interactive tool.** Too often presenters put up a chart on a slide without thinking about how to engage the audience. For example, look at the chart below, which depicts volume of sales per quarter (in millions):

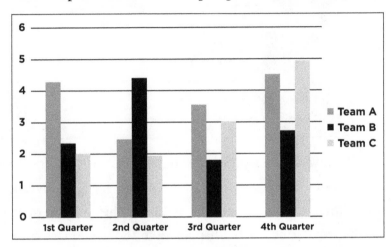

If you show this chart to your audience, they will quickly figure out for themselves what kind of progress (or lack of progress) the three teams have made in a year. While you are still talking about what happened in the first quarter ("Team A established an early lead, with Teams B and C lagging behind"), your audience is already looking at the fourth quarter and thinking, "Team A turned in a similar performance, while Team C surged ahead significantly." Then they will likely stop listening to you and engage themselves with their smart phones.

To involve the audience in the discussion of charts such as this one, don't show them the whole chart at once. Rather, on one slide, place the chart with just the first-quarter results, like so:

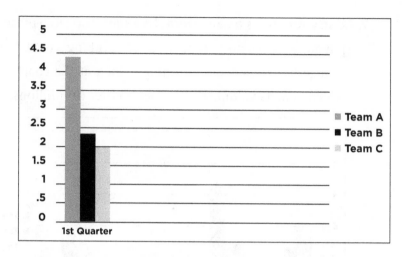

Now the audience can't jump ahead of you, and they will listen more carefully to what you have to say about the first-quarter results. In addition, they will most likely be wondering, "What happened in the next quarter?" You will have built up the suspense, which is often an effective way to involve the audience.

You can use this technique with any kind of chart, whether it be a bar chart, a column chart (like the one above), a pie chart, or any chart that shows information across time. Use the animation power of PowerPoint[32] or other visual tools to stir your audience's interest in what you have to say.

For more examples of how to engage your audience, look at the "interactive lectures" that Thiagi has included on his website, www.thiagi.com. According to Thiagi, "Interactive lectures involve participants in the learning process while providing complete control to the instructor. These activities enable a

---

[32]For more detailed instructions on how to animate charts in PowerPoint, visit Dave Paradi's website: http://www.thinkoutsidetheslide.com.

quick and easy conversion of a passive presentation into an interactive experience. Different types of interactive lectures incorporate built-in quizzes, interspersed tasks, teamwork interludes, and participant control of the presentation."[33]

It can be very effective (and powerful) if you resist the urge to do *all* of the talking. By sharing the stage, you increase the audience's engagement while reducing the burden on yourself. Who wouldn't want that?

---

[33] Thiagarajan, Sivasailam. "Mixed-Up Sentences." The Thiagi Group. January 13, 2015. http://www.thiagi.com/archived-games/2015/1/13/mixed-up-sentences.

Chapter 9

Rehearse Repeatedly to Sound Spontaneous

*Success depends upon previous preparation, and
without such preparation there is sure to be failure.*

CONFUCIUS

Y ou might think that in order to prepare for a presentation
in English, you should write out your entire presentation on
sheets of paper, or note cards, or on your slides.

You might think that—but you should not do it.[34] A scripted
presentation may make things easier for you, but it will almost
certainly make it more difficult for your audience. For one thing, if
you keep your eyes focused on your notes or your slides, you will
make no eye contact with the audience, thus disengaging yourself
from them. For another, most audience members (children are
exceptions) detest it when other people read to them, and they will
tune you out fairly quickly and look for more interesting things to

[34]Note: A scripted presentation will be effective only if you are giving a speech in a situation where you
are expected to do all the talking, and the audience responds only by applauding or perhaps laughing.
Examples would be the president of the United States giving the State of the Union Address to the
assembled members of congress (and the millions of citizens at home watching on their TVs) or the
president of China giving a welcome speech at the Boao Forum of Asia to the forum participants
(and the millions of citizens at home watching on their TVs). In such situations, a professional speech
writer will most likely write the speech, which the speaker will review and then practice. An effective
speaker will be able to read the speech while making frequent eye contact with the audience, as
Xi Jinping does in this speech [https://www.youtube.com/watch?v=CdiOD2MJQZQ] and as Barack
Obama does in this speech [https://www.youtube.com/watch?v=Z8LqG_Ld0Dw].

do. A successful presentation should be a shared experience between you and your audience; if you read to them, you will be delivering a one-sided, one-directional lecture. For nonnative English speakers, it might feel comforting to give a fully scripted presentation that has all of the "right words" written down; however, it is usually more effective to sacrifice a little bit of language accuracy for a lot of audience engagement, connection, and rapport.

So, if it's not a good idea to write out your entire presentation, what should you do? If you want your presentation to sound spontaneous—as though you were thinking about and saying your ideas for the very first time—you need to organize your presentation around key words. Think *notes*, not *script*. You can write your key words on sheets of paper that you place flat on a surface in front of you so that you can see them but your audience can't, or on your slides. Let us stress again that you are writing only key words—not sentences, not paragraphs. For example, here are before (on the left) and after (on the right) slides from a presentation called "Managing Performance: What Works?"

II. Identifying Performance Problems	II. Identifying Performance Problems
• NPT = Measurable Goals and Current Performance; Analyze Cause of Gaps, Solutions; Implementation & Assessment • We defeat process by not analyzing the cause of gaps • We impulsively select solutions that 2/3 of the time either have no result or make things worse	• NPT = Measurable Goals and Current Performance • Gap Analysis • Best Solutions

Notice that the left-hand slide has not only too many words, it also has complete sentences. A good guideline for slides is six words per bullet and six bullets per slide, and no complete sentences unless you're citing a direct quotation. The slide on the left will make it very tempting for you to want to read the slide to your audience, most of whom will finish reading the entire slide before you do. The slide on the right, by contrast, includes only a few key words, for which the audience will need to listen to the explanations that you provide. In other words, *you* should describe what gap analysis is and not rely on the slide to do all the talking for you.

Another advantage to a more extemporaneous approach to making a presentation is that it will allow you to be much more flexible. Suppose, for example, that one of your audience members interrupts you to ask a question or make a comment. (And suppose that the person who does so is a senior executive of the company you work for.) If you are reading from a *script*, such an interruption may derail your concentration and make it very difficult for you to get back into the correct rhythm after you have dealt with the interruption. If you are speaking from *notes*, on the other hand, such interruptions will not throw you off course—in fact, you will welcome such responses from your audience, as they will indicate people are really listening to you and wanting to participate. Additionally, if you are speaking from notes, you can adjust your timing by deleting any points that may not be necessary to the overall presentation. If you are speaking from a script, you won't be able to make such adjustments without awkwardness. You might think that producing a scripted presentation will give you more control, but in reality, it will give you less.

An even better approach is to use more pictures on your slides than text. This way, you can speak about each image for as long as you like (or as your time limit allows), explaining it in ways that you consider most useful for your particular audience. For nonnative English speakers, using pictures can be an especially helpful way to make your point without worrying about getting the wording exactly right. Why wrestle with finding the perfect language to explain gap analysis, for example, when you can show the audience a chart or an image that reinforces your key message, and then allows for a discussion:

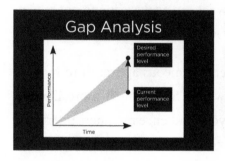

Still one more advantage of speaking from notes is that this method will allow you to insert anecdotes, personal stories, analogies, and examples whenever you feel the need, based on your audience's reactions to your presentation. (You won't be able to judge their reaction if you focus solely on your script without making eye contact with anyone.)

For example, in the "Managing Performance" presentation, a presenter who speaks from notes and slides with key words or images would be able to tell a personal story about a firsthand experience with a company that was having difficulties managing the performance of its employees (as time allows and as the audience responds). Remember that stories are universally effective for capturing and maintaining an audience's attention. As we mentioned in chapter 3, stories are also an opportunity for you to share more about your country, culture, upbringing, or perspective with your listeners, and thus build trust and connection.

Another advantage of using notes is that you will be better able to deal with any problems that might occur during your presentation. If your laptop decides to die in the middle, you can continue speaking from your notes. If the company suddenly stages a fire drill during your presentation, you can figure out how to adjust your remarks during the break and get right back to where you need to be when the drill is over. If you suddenly realize, five minutes into your presentation, that the wrong audience is present (you thought you would be presenting to representatives of the U.S. Air Force about the latest in missile defense systems; the audience members turn out to be junior high school students on a field trip—this actually happened to a speaker author Ellen knows personally), you can start over from a place where both you and the unanticipated audience will feel comfortable.

While Deborah has a background in improvisation and rarely uses notes in her presentations, she does have ten tips for how to hold and reference hand-held notes so that you're still connecting with the audience more than you're connecting to a piece of paper.

Using Hand-Held Notes

1. Make sure any hand-held notes look crisp and professional from the audience's perspective. Don't bring a stack of crumpled papers with you; it will undermine your credibility. Use clean pieces of white computer paper or index cards, on which the ink isn't visible from the back of the page.

2. Write your notes in large enough font that you can simply

glance at them and access the information you need. You don't want to be squinting and scanning the page for the next thing you're trying to say.

3. Write large page numbers on each sheet of paper or index card. That way, if they get shuffled or out of order, you can quickly find your place.

4. If your presentation requires you to stand at a lectern, practice delivering the presentation so that you're referencing your notes as rarely as possible. Your rehearsal should also prepare you for when you move to the next page. Avoid turning pages in the middle of an important idea, a quotation or a story. Look for natural breaks between main points to turn the page.

5. If you're going to be moving during the presentation (which we highly recommend), put your notes down on a table or a lectern when you're not using them, as long as you won't need them frequently. It's more distracting to watch you keep walking over to pick them up from a table then for you to just hold them in one hand.

6. When you're using notes, hold them in your non-dominant hand (so in your left hand if you are a "righty," and in your right hand if you are a "lefty"). Anchor that elbow to your waist and hold your notes firmly, with limited movement. Use your other hand to gesture. Don't gesture with the hand holding your notes—the flapping paper will be a distraction to your audience.

7. Don't read your notes while speaking. Look at your notes, scan them quickly, and then turn your eye contact back to the audience and resume speaking. Otherwise you'll look like your audience is your stack of index cards.

8. An exception to "don't read your notes" is when you want to make it clear that you're deliberately reading for the sake of accuracy, such as offering an important statistic or a direct quotation. You might even signal this to the audience by saying something like, "I'd like to read our Vision Statement aloud so that we're all clear on where we're going."

9. Think of your notes as a bright shiny object. Chances are your eyes and your audience's eyes will be drawn to those notes, unless you use them carefully, strategically, and infrequently, and make up for the use of notes with powerful body language and vocal variety.

10. Many presenters discover that their notes are like a security blanket—they thought they needed them for comfort and reassurance, but they realized that they never looked at them throughout the presentation. If you don't need them, don't use them.

Mark Twain once said: "It usually takes me more than three weeks to prepare a good impromptu speech." Make sure you put the time, energy, and effort into looking and sounding comfortable, prepared, and confident.

Chapter 10

Respect Gender Roles

One child must never be set above another, even in casual conversation, not to mention in speeches that circle the globe.

AUTHOR ALICE WALKER

It has not been an easy journey for Americans and people from other Western countries to come to terms with the concept of gender equality. For too many years to count, stereotypes have existed that paint all women and all men with one large indiscriminating brush. Here are a few of them (from the *List of Gender Stereotypes*[35] by Holly Brewer):

- Women are weaker than men physically.

- Women don't play sports.

- Women are not politicians.

- Men do not cook, sew, or do crafts.

- Men are lazy and/or messy.

- Men enjoy outdoor activities such as camping, fishing, and hiking.

[35] Brewer, Holly. "List of Gender Stereotypes." HealthGuidance.org. Accessed February 26, 2017. http://www.healthguidance.org/entry/15910/1/List-of-Gender-Stereotypes.html.

Just as recently as 2016, an incident occurred on a jet plane in which a passenger had a medical emergency midflight, and a flight attendant asked if there was a doctor on board. A black female passenger stood up and said, "I'm a doctor." (She was an obstetrician—a real doctor.) The flight attendant would not believe that she could be a doctor and asked to see her credentials. (Because doctors are always men, right?)

Just because incidents like this continue to occur, it doesn't mean that Westerners aren't concerned about overcoming such blatant gender bias. Especially in language, we have tried to become more inclusive in what we say and how we say it. So, when you are speaking to a Western audience, you need to be mindful of how sensitive Westerners can be to gender stereotyping.

Here are six ways to be sure that you do not exclude members of any gender from your audiences (from The *Handbook of Nonsexist Writing* by Casey Miller, Kate Swift, and Kate Mosse):[36]

1. **Avoid the generic use of the word "man."** For example, instead of saying, "Ever since the dawn of civilization, man has attempted to expand his horizons and learn new things," say, "Ever since the dawn of civilization, humans have attempted to expand their horizons and learn new things."

2. **Use the plural, non-specific gender form of the personal pronoun.** For example, instead of saying, "When a new supervisor encounters a problem, he usually asks his mentor for advice," say, "When new supervisors encounter a problem, they usually ask their mentors for advice."

---

[36]Miller, Casey, Kate Swift, and Kate Mosse. *The Handbook of Nonsexist Writing for Writers, Editors, and Speakers*. London: Women's Press, 1995.

3. **Search for alternatives to male-oriented job positions.** For example, change "warehouse foreman" to "warehouse supervisor or manager;" "salesman" to "sales agent or representative;" and "cameraman" to "camera operator."

4. **Use "he or she" when referring to positions of power in society.** For example, don't say, "When a person becomes president of the United States, he is faced with the daunting task of unifying two diverse political parties." Change the pronoun: "When a person becomes president of the United States, he or she . . . ," thus reinforcing the idea that anyone, male or female, can potentially become president.

5. **Be completely consistent with social titles.** In a group presentation, do not address the male speaker as "Mr. Chen" and the female speaker as "Iris." (Use either "Mr. Chen" and "Ms. Li" or "Bo" and "Iris.")

6. **Avoid references to the physical body (unless, of course, your presentation is about the physical body).** Don't introduce your speaking partner as "handsome" or "beautiful." Stick to their professional qualifications, not their physical attributes (Ellen once had a Chinese student who introduced his obviously pregnant female partner by saying, "Lily will bring a warm quality to this presentation because she is going to have a baby!" Deborah had a male client from Hong Kong who introduced his female colleague as "sexy"—a lawsuit waiting to happen.)

We all have some gender bias, no matter what culture we are from. If a man gets up to speak, do you pay more attention to his remarks simply because he is a male? If a woman does likewise, do you tend to discount her opinions to some degree, simply because she is female?

A Lumen Learning course on public speaking addressed gender bias in this way: "Taking a step back and considering what gender bias you bring to the table, as well as what gender biases your audience might have of you is an important step in eliminating or at least addressing gender bias in your speech."

Gender bias may still be a reality in many cultures and companies, but it doesn't have to be reflected in your presentation.

Chapter 11

Become Culturally Aware

To effectively communicate, we must realize that we are all different in the way we perceive the world and use this understanding as a guide to our communication with others.

MOTIVATIONAL SPEAKER TONY ROBBINS

n his book, *Leading with Cultural Intelligence: The Real Secret to Success*, author David A. Livermore defines cultural intelligence as "the capability to function effectively across national, ethnic, and organizational cultures."[37]

Professor Michelle LeBaron, author of *Bridging Cultural Conflicts: A New Approach for a Changing World* tells us, "All communication is cultural: it draws on ways we have learned to speak and give nonverbal messages."[38]

That being said, you can still improve the impact of your presentations by understanding the general expectations of many Western, English-speaking audiences. (And when we say "general expectations," we mean exactly that. It still pays to do your research ahead of time,

---

[37] Livermore, David A. *Leading with Cultural Intelligence: The Real Secret to Success.* New York, NY: American Management Association, 2015.

[38] LeBaron, Michelle. *Bridging Cultural Conflicts: A New Approach for a Changing World.* San Francisco, CA: John Wiley, 2004.

and to read the room so you can make adjustments while you are speaking.)

In chapter 6, we addressed how emotionally expressive certain cultures tend to be, with Americans rated high, based on their collective history of migration. Erin Meyer, author of *The Culture Map: Breaking Through the Invisible Boundaries of Global Business*[39] and Andy Molinsky, author of *Global Dexterity: How to Adapt Your Business Across Cultures Without Losing Yourself in the Process*[40] both highlight several other factors to consider in comparing your native culture's typical approach versus a typical American approach.

- **Communicating: Explicit versus Implicit.** Meyer's research shows that Americans have the most explicit culture; therefore, your presentations should be precise, simple, and clear. Say exactly what you mean, and don't leave your message open to interpretation or inference. Repeat key messages to ensure understanding. Molinsky addresses a related cultural factor which he calls *Directness*, meaning how straightforward you can be. An American audience will most likely want you to get right to the point and stop wasting their time by "beating around the bush." On the other hand, American audiences also respond well to personal examples, as long as they are relevant, reinforce the key point and are short. A good guideline for a story's length is 90 seconds or less.

---

[39]Meyer, Erin. *The Culture Map: Breaking through the Invisible Boundaries of Global Business.* New York: Public Affairs, 2014.

[40]Molinsky, Andy. *Global Dexterity: How to Adapt Your Behavior Across Cultures without Losing Yourself in the Process.* Boston: Harvard Business Review Press, 2013.

- **Evaluating: Direct Negative Feedback versus Indirect Negative Feedback.** Americans are in the middle of the spectrum when it comes to giving and receiving negative feedback, writes Meyer. If your presentation includes negative feedback, you might need to be slightly less direct than you would in other parts of your presentation. Consider including the upside of the negative feedback and helpful and practical suggestions regarding how to improve these specific areas. Negative feedback should also, when possible, be delivered privately rather than in a public group presentation setting.

- **Persuading: Deductive Argument versus Inductive Argument.** Americans (along with people from Canada, the United Kingdom, and Australia) prefer presentations that begin with a fact, statement, or opinion, and then back it up with supporting evidence for the conclusion. This is why the *Objective* section of your presentation should come directly after a brief *Opening*—you want to get the audience's attention and then keep it by letting them know exactly what your point is. Expect discussions to be practical, tactical, and direct, rather than theoretical or philosophical; thus, you should prepare practical, tactical, and direct answers to the questions that may arise.

- **Self-Promotion: I versus We.** Americans tend to score high on Molinsky's variable of Self-promotion, meaning that when you give a persuasive presentation, you will be expected to speak positively about yourself, and to promote your qualifications. Individual self-promotion, when done in context, is considered a sign of competence and confidence.

- **Leading: Egalitarian versus Hierarchical.** Meyer's research shows that Americans tend to have a moderate stance on whether communication must respect, or can skip, hierarchical lines. You might find yourself presenting to a mixed group of professionals in a single meeting that includes executives, midlevel managers and line staff, all together. As always, it helps to ask ahead of time what levels will be in the room or to do a quick survey in the room if you can't find out in advance. Molinsky addresses a related factor, which he calls *Formality*, which determines how much deference and respect you should display in your communication style. Most American audiences prefer a laid-back, rather than formal atmosphere, but in reality, the style will depend mostly on the culture of a particular organization. If you are speaking to software engineers who work for a technology firm, you may need to dress informally (polo shirts and khaki slacks or colorful blouses and simple skirts—and maybe even clean jeans) to mirror your audience's style. If you are speaking to corporate lawyers, you will probably need to dress more formally (suit and tie; jacket and blouse with skirt or trousers). If the CEO of Intel (Brian Krzanich, as of this writing) is present, you may be fine addressing him as "Brian." If a member of your audience is a United States Supreme Court justice, it would be best to address him as "Chief Justice Roberts," rather than "John."

- **Deciding: Consensual versus Top-Down.** Similar to their attitudes on leading, Americans also score toward the middle of the scale when it comes to deciding, between consensual and top-down (with a slight leaning toward top-down). This means your content and your messaging should address a wide range of decision rights within the group. It also means that you will want to ask ahead of time (or in the room, if necessary) how and by whom decisions about your proposal will be made.

- **Trusting: Task versus Relationship.** For Americans, according to Meyer, many business relationships are built on practicality and task completion rather than on slowly and gradually cultivating a relationship over time. Thus, you may find yourself needing to make presentations that sell or aim to influence people with whom you have little to no previous personal relationship, familiarity, or connection. You might also need to be prepared to make a request of people before you feel really comfortable. In addition, others might decide whether or not they trust you based on your business competence and reliability, so include information that highlights your credibility in your presentation. Despite this task-first mentality, Americans tend to score high on Molinsky's *Personal Disclosure* variable. American audiences usually respond well to personal stories and anecdotes. Indeed, such a disclosure tends to be more persuasive than just listing facts and figures, and builds trust. Many of the greatest speeches made by famous Americans include personal disclosure to connect with the audience and add a touch of humanity. For example, take the case of baseball player Lou Gehrig, who was forced to retire from playing with the New York Yankees because he had contracted what is now known as Lou Gehrig's Disease (amyotrophic lateral sclerosis). In 1939, he made an impassioned speech to the assembled fans in Yankee Stadium in which he referred to himself as "the luckiest man on the face of this earth" because, "when you have a wonderful mother-in-law who takes sides with you in squabbles with her own daughter—that's something. When you have a father and a mother who work all their lives so that you can have an education and build your body—it's a blessing. When you have a wife who has been a tower of strength and shown more courage than you dreamed existed—that's the finest I know."

Americans perceive the sharing of personal information, no matter how painful, to be a sign of courage, as long as you can stay in control of your emotions. So, go ahead and tell stories about your own personal experiences with your product or your position. Be brave.

- **Disagreeing: Confrontational versus Avoiding Confrontation.** Yet again, American audiences are in the middle between considering open disagreement and debate healthy for a team as opposed to believing that it could negatively impact relationships and shouldn't be done publicly (if it all). As a presenter, you will need to assess your audience to see whether they're comfortable making challenging statements or asking questions that debate your key messages. Molinsky advocates for looking at *Assertiveness*, where a speaker needs to navigate how strongly he or she may voice a personal opinion and endorse a particular point of view. While not all Americans want a fight (especially a public one), most Americans will expect you to stand up for your proposition. Do not weaken your own argument by downplaying its importance by saying such things as, "Well, it's only my opinion," "Of course I could be wrong," "It's okay if you want to disagree," etc. If you act like an expert, the audience will be more inclined to accept you as such. This is related to *Enthusiasm*, another cultural factor described by Molinsky. How much emotion and energy should you show when communicating to Americans? While you don't want to scream, cry, do a "happy dance," or laugh uncontrollably, Americans tend to place a high value on how personally invested the speaker is in his or her subject. You will need to demonstrate both your enthusiasm for your message and your belief that your proposal is the best means to achieve the best end, verbally, vocally, and visually.

- **Scheduling: Linear versus Flexible.** More often than not, Americans approach projects in a linear, sequential manner, regarding interruptions or midcourse changes as something to be avoided. Deadlines and schedules are held in high regard. When you make a presentation, offer a linear, sequential, step-by-step approach in which you clearly address the schedule and offer solutions in advance of anticipated setbacks. A high value on linear processes also means that your presentation should end when it's supposed to end—not five to ten minutes after people expect you to be finished.

As you can see, preparing to present in English as a nonnative English speaker requires a little research, a lot of self-awareness, and massive amounts of flexibility. As mogul Richard Branson put it: "Every success story is a tale of constant adaption, revision, and change." And every successful presentation is, too.

Chapter 12

Master Questions and Answers with Ease and Confidence

Culture makes people understand each other better. And if they understand each other better in their soul, it is easier to overcome the economic and political barriers. But first they have to understand that their neighbor is, in the end, just like them, with the same problems, the same questions.

PAULO COELHO, THE ALCHEMIST

One of Deborah's favorite cartoons depicts a speaker at a lectern with the caption, "That concludes the annual report. I will now fend off questions from the stockholders."

Most presenters—no matter what language they speak—tend to think of taking questions from the audience as a high-risk, low-reward endeavor. You've spent all that time preparing a presentation—why should you expose yourself to potential criticism or to someone questioning your approach? Can't everyone just applaud and leave?

That might be nice in theory, but in reality, questions from the audience tend to offer more opportunities than obstacles. What opportunities? Opportunities to create buy-in, to guide the participants in a rich discussion, to get new (and possibly improved) approaches and perspectives, and to connect and engage with your audience. Questions help your listeners focus their thinking so they can convince themselves.

So, there is little question that your presentation will benefit from some Q&A. And there is *no* question that you need to be prepared for Q&A. One way to be prepared is to let your audience know proactively how and when you will take questions. Will you take them from the beginning and throughout? Should they save them for the formal Q&A period? No matter what ground rules you set at the beginning, be aware that audience members may interrupt you to ask a question or to comment (or to criticize). You must prepare for such interruptions to ensure that you do not become rattled and lose your train of thought.

There are (at least) eight questions that you can and need to ask yourself that will help you enter the Q&A portion of your presentation with greater confidence. And if you're thinking strategically, you will build some of these answers into the presentation itself so that, if the question arises, you can say, "As I mentioned earlier . . ." (Wouldn't that feel great?)

- **What is most important and relevant about my topic for this audience?** In other words, think about the WIIFM ("What's In It For Me?") for this audience, and make sure to address that throughout. Addressing it once will not be enough, as audiences often disengage when you're not speaking directly about their needs and interests.

- **How does what I am proposing fit into the bigger picture?** Your listeners have their own priorities and obligations, so let them know how what you're pitching integrates with, reinforces, and leverages their goals, projects, and plans.

- **How easy can I make this for them?** You may think that the idea you're pitching is an easy decision. Great—make sure you are very clear in demonstrating the feasibility of turning your idea into action.

- **What's this going to cost?** Show them the money, but also remember that costs extend beyond dollars and cents. Be clear and up front about costs of personnel, energy, time and other valuable resources, and include your perspective on what makes this worth it, or not (if that's your angle).

- **When will this all happen?** Timing is everything. Share as much as you can about when the proposed project will start and end, and milestones along the way.

- **Who is in charge?** If you're making the presentation, there's often an assumption that you're the one carrying out the work. If that's so, make a case for why you have the competence and credibility to do so. If it's not you, let the listeners know who is doing what, and why that person or team is well positioned to succeed.

- **What's my stake in this?** Sure, we all have to make presentations from time to time where we're not really feeling invested in it, but the more you can let your audience understand not just how much you know but how much you care, what your stake is, and your unique perspective on it, the greater credibility you bring to the presentation.

- **How can I view the Q&A as something positive?** If you can convince yourself to look forward to the audience's questions (because you believe that their inquiries will build trust with you, especially when you handle them well), the end result will be to focus their thinking and your own, guide a rich discussion, discover better answers than you might have come up with yourself, and contribute to shared ownership of the topic or project under discussion.

If you have planned for an official Q&A at the end (and if your audience respects your wishes to hold their comments until then), this section of your presentation will also provide a good opportunity for you to maintain and expand on the rapport you established early in your presentation—but only if you manage it effectively:

1. **Ask for questions and wait.** (Some professional speakers advise that you wait at least nine seconds before giving up and saying, "All right, so if there are no questions, here is my conclusion. . . .") some audience members might not be ready yet and need a second or two to respond. Look around the room, making brief eye contact with as many people as possible. If you see someone who appears ready to speak, give that person a little nod of encouragement. Let your audience know that it's safe to speak up. Sometimes it is a good idea to plant a question or two with a friendly member of the audience to get the process started. Once someone asks a

question, often other audience members feel encouraged to ask one too.

2. **While someone is asking a question, really listen to it.** Focus all your attention on the question; move closer to the questioner to make sure that you hear it correctly. Make the questioner feel that he or she is the only person in the room.

3. **Determine what kind of question this is.** Not all questions are the same, and you want to listen to both the content of the question and the goal of the questioner. Some questions are informational—they're seeking additional data, facts, timing, budget, etc. Examples include questions like: "When is the plant inspection scheduled?" or, "How many salespeople will you be training in the third quarter?" Other questions are speculative, asking you reflect beyond the facts, and include your opinion. Examples of speculative questions include: "How do you think this technology will change over the next ten years?" or, "What new regulations are likely to impact our industry in the coming months?" You might also face hostile questions (hopefully not very often), the goals of which include allowing the questioner to express his or her opinions or emotions in an aggressive (or passive-aggressive) way, showing off his or her knowledge or experience at the expense of the speaker, and/or simply embarrassing the speaker. Examples of these include, "Don't you think you should have considered all stakeholder groups before you put this plan into place?" or, "Isn't this ad campaign just another misguided attempt to attract millennials?"

4. **Once you've heard the question, paraphrase it for the rest of the audience.** You might say, "Let me make sure I understand your question. It sounds like you're asking [rephrase their question in your own words]. Is that right?" A paraphrase has several benefits:

    - It ensures that all members of the audience actually hear the question. This is particularly important if the questioner is in the front row.

    - It allows you to confirm that you understood the question. The questioner should indicate "yes" or "no" after your paraphrase.

    - It may defuse any hostility the questioner may have toward you since you will both have to agree that you understand the question.

    - It buys you time while you try to figure out an answer.

5. **Remember that individuals ask the questions, but the *group* needs the answers.** As you begin to answer the question, make eye contact with the questioner for a few moments, then break away and make eye contact with the entire audience.

6. **Align your answer with the kind of question being asked.** If the question is informational, provide the information. What if you don't know the answer to the question? It's all right to say "I don't know." You can then assure the questioner that you'll follow up and get back to them with a response as soon as possible. Then quickly steer the focus back to a point you *do* know.

If the question calls for you to speculate, don't guess—analyze or abstain. In other words, if you're deeply knowledgeable about online marketing, and you're asked to speculate on future trends in online marketing, you can share your analysis of where you think the industry is heading. You should acknowledge aloud that you've been asked to speculate ("It sounds like you're asking me to speculate on where the industry is heading—is that right?") and that you are doing so based on your analysis of the past and present, and not knowledge of the future. ("While none of us can know the future for sure, based on past and current trends, I would speculate that . . .") If you can't reasonably speculate, or you feel like the risk of getting it wrong is too high or could cause too much damage down the road, abstain from speculating. Use the opportunity to reinforce a key point or message. You might say, "I can't speculate on where the industry is heading, but what I can tell you is that we have a tremendous opportunity right now to shape our future direction. As I mentioned in my presentation . . ." and then reinforce your key message.

7. **When you are finished answering the question, make eye contact with the questioner again and say, "Does that answer your question?"** If the questioner says no, then try the whole process again. Then open it up to the audience as a whole again. You can also offer the question to the audience to answer. (This technique is often used by college professors, and it has the added benefit of stimulating audience interaction).

Let's pause for a moment to consider what you should do if you get a hostile question: Don't take the bait. Don't get angry. And don't get defensive. You want to make sure that a hostile questioner doesn't get the attention, focus, or compassion of the audience. You also want to make sure that a hostile questioner doesn't sway the audience, or undermine your authority and confidence. Here are five techniques you can try:

- **Acknowledge the reason for the emotion, but not the emotion itself.** Imagine being asked this question: "Why doesn't management seem to care about our union workers?" Don't say, "Wow, you sound furious!" unless you want to risk the questioner responding, "Damn right, I'm furious! And you want to know why? Because of you people . . ." and then taking over the presentation. You might try saying, "It sounds like union workers are critically important to you. Let me stress how critically important they are to us, too. With that shared objective, I'd like to address . . ."

- **Act a bit confused to buy some time and space for both of you.** Assume that when people are hostile, they are less likely to communicate clearly and understandably. You can also use your nonnative English speaking to your advantage here. If someone is angry or aggressive in their questioning, take a moment and say, "I didn't quite understand the question you're asking. Would you please ask it another way?" It will, in many cases, force the questioner to stop his or her attack, and think about rewording the question in a way that is less heated. It also might prompt the questioner to realize that he or she was actually making a statement, and not really asking a question. For example, if the questioner originally asked, "Why doesn't management seem to care about our union workers?" you might ask for a rewording or for clarification. The questioner might realize that he or she was actually making a statement in the form of a question—"It seems like management doesn't care about our union workers"—and then go ahead and make that statement (which you can then address) or drop it altogether.

- **Ignore the tone and answer the question.** Just because the question sounded hostile doesn't mean that you need to continue adding to its tone. Imagine, once again, this question coming at you in an angry tone: "Why doesn't management seem to care about our union workers?" You can calmly answer, "In terms of management's care for our union workers, let me share with you what we've done toward that over the last year."

- **Speak only for yourself.** Hostile question: "Why doesn't management seem to care about our union workers?"

  You: "While I can't speak for all managers, I can tell you what I have done toward that over the past year. First of all, I . . ."

- **Dodge it and deliver an eloquent (but somewhat tangential) response.** In their article in the *Journal of Experimental Psychology*, "The Artful Dodger: Answering the Wrong Question the Right Way,"[41] researchers Todd Rogers and Michael I. Norton point out that listeners

[41] Rogers, Todd, and Michael I. Norton. "The Artful Dodger: Answering the Wrong Question the Right Way." *Journal of Experimental Psychology: Applied* 17, no. 2 (2011): 139-47. doi:10.1037/a0023439.

tend to be more impressed with speakers who artfully and eloquently sidestep the question being asked than they are with speakers who offer a direct answer that is inarticulate. Short attention spans are to blame here—if you can address a question with a related response, and do it with confidence and conviction, the questioner is likely to forget exactly what he or she originally asked. (We think that this is another excellent reason to improve your overall presentation skills.)

With lots of audience analysis and preparation before the presentation, you should significantly decrease the odds that an audience member will ask a question that you can't answer. And with lots of confidence and conviction, you can increase the odds that when you do answer a question, the listener will be satisfied, and move on. Chances are, you'll feel satisfied, too.

Afterword

We hope that you have learned many useful techniques to help you increase your confidence, competence, and cultural comfort that you can use immediately in your very next presentation. Sometimes all it takes is a small change here or a minor adjustment there to see real improvement. In other cases, however, you will need to devote significant time and energy to becoming a masterful presenter—which is true in any language.

Whether you anticipate needing to do a little work or a lot, remember that having a solid design structure for your presentation will increase your confidence. Additionally, establishing rapport with your audience will help you overcome stage fright. Don't forget that simplifying your English vocabulary will make your presentations more memorable and that using appropriate and powerful gestures and movement will make you more persuasive. Keep in mind that modulating your speaking voice will help keep your audience awake and involved. Becoming aware of cultural differences and gender roles will help you come across as a credible and trustworthy professional.

And the best news of all? Keep working at presenting and eventually you will find it a pleasure to present in English because your message will shine through loud and clear.

Are there any questions? (Pause for response.)

If so, let us know by visiting us at www.TipsoftheTongue.com, where you will find additional tools, videos and resources, or e-mail us at Help@TipsoftheTongue.com.

In closing, just remember the words of American film director John Ford: "You can speak well if your tongue can deliver the message of your heart."

To your speaking success,

—Deborah Grayson Riegel and Ellen Dowling

About the Authors

Deborah Grayson Riegel is the CEO and Chief Communication Coach for Talk Support, and the Director of Learning for The Boda Group. She started her career at age seventeen, when she won a national championship in public speaking as a high school senior in New York City, and was immediately recruited to coach on presentation and communication skills at colleges and corporations. Deborah earned a bachelor's degree in psychology from the University of Michigan and a master's degree in social work from Columbia University, supporting herself by performing improvisation and stand-up comedy. Deborah is a lecturer of management communication at the Wharton School of The University of Pennsylvania. She also served as a visiting professor of executive communications at the Beijing International MBA Program at Peking University, China. Deborah's clients have ranged from Kraft Foods, Monster Worldwide and Pfizer to The American Bar Association, Fox and The United States Army. She has been a featured expert and a contributor to *Harvard Business Review, The New York Times, Oprah Magazine, Forbes, Fast Company, Bloomberg BusinessWeek, Fox Business Network*, and *American Express OPEN Small Business Forum*. She and her husband, Michael, are the proud parents of twins, Jacob and Sophie, who are quickly becoming better public speakers than she is.

E llen Dowling, Ph.D., president of Dowling & Associates, Inc., has consulted with many organizations in communication skills, management development, and organizational development. She is a nationally recognized expert on training design and delivery and an internationally known speaker and trainer. Her clients in the United States include Honeywell, Intel Corporation, Alltel, Lockheed Martin, and Sandia National Laboratories. Her clients in China include Pfizer, the State Food and Drug Administration, and the National Development and Reform Commission. From 2006 to 2014, she was a visiting professor in the Beijing International MBA Program at Peking University, where she taught report writing and presentation skills to international MBA candidates. She is the author of *The Standup Trainer* and co-author of *Presenting with Style: Advanced Strategies for Superior Presentations.* In her spare time, she is president and newsletter editor of the Irish-American Society of New Mexico. She is also studying Chinese.

Works Referenced

"40 Brilliant Idioms That Simply Can't Be Translated Literally." TED Blog. August 10, 2015. http://blog.ted.com/40-idioms-that-cant-be-translated-literally/.

"Achieve Accent Neutralization." Accessed February 24, 2017. http://www.wikihow.com/Achieve-Accent-Neutralization.

Allende, Isabel. "Tales of Passion." Isabel Allende: Tales of Passion | TED Talk | TED.com. Accessed February 23, 2017. http://www.ted.com/talks/isabel_allende_tells_tales_of_passion.

Angela Merkel Speaking English to British Parliament. Performed by Angela Merkel. February 28, 2014. https://www.youtube.com/watch?v=cGZWR5S1lCo.

Barrault, Jean-Louis. "Child of Silence." Translated by Eric Bentley. In *Theatre Arts on Acting*, edited by Laurence Senelick. London: Routledge, 2008.

Beck, Megan and Barry Libert. "The Rise of AI Makes Emotional Intelligence More Important." Harvard Business Review. February 15, 2017. https://hbr.org/2017/02/the-rise-of-ai-makes-emotional-intelligence-more-important.

Braithwaite, Lisa. "Lecture vs. Presentation." Speak Schmeak. September 9, 2011. http://www.speakschmeak.com/2011/09/lecture-vs-presentation.html.

Bradberry, Travis, Jean Greaves, and Patrick Lencioni. *Emotional Intelligence 2.0: The World's Most Popular Emotional Intelligence Test.* San Diego (California): TalentSmart, 2009.

Brewer, Holly. "List of Gender Stereotypes." HealthGuidance. org. Accessed February 26, 2017. http://www.healthguidance.org/entry/15910/1/List-of-Gender-Stereotypes.html.

"Business Buzzwords Generator - WSJ.com." *The Wall Street Journal.* Accessed February 24, 2017. http://projects.wsj.com/buzzwords2014 /#p=7|31,4|32|0|||0.

"Business Jargon Is Not a Value-Add." *Harvard Business Review.* March 30, 2015. https://hbr.org/2011/12/business-jargon-is-not-a-value.

Cuddy, Amy, Matthew Kohut, and John Neffinger. "Connect, Then Lead." *Harvard Business Review.* November 02, 2014. Accessed February 26, 2017. https://hbr.org/2013/07/connect-then-lead.

Cuddy, Amy. *Presence: Bringing Your Boldest Self to Your Biggest Challenges.* St. Louis: Little, Brown, 2017.

Cuddy, Amy. "Your Body Language Shapes Who You Are." Amy Cuddy: Your Body Language Shapes Who You Are | TED Talk | TED.com. June 2012. https://www.ted.com/talks/amy_cuddy_your_body_language_shapes_who_you_are.

Dickens, Charles. *A Tale of Two Cities.* Upper Saddle River, NJ: Prentice Hall, 1991.

Engen, Kristin J. Van, and Jonathan E. Peelle. "Listening Effort and Accented Speech." *Frontiers in Human Neuroscience* 8 (2014).

"Gender Bias in Public Speaking." Gender Bias: Public Speaking/ Speech Communication. Accessed February 26, 2017. https://lumen. instructure.com/courses/218897/pages/linkedtext54261.

Goleman, Daniel. *Emotional Intelligence: Why It Can Matter More than IQ.* London: Bloomsbury, 2010.

Hettiarachchi, Dananjaya. "Dananjaya Hettiarachchi World Champion of Public Speaking 2014 - Full Speech." YouTube. September 22, 2014. https://youtu.be/bbz2boNSeL0.

"IMac G4 Unveiling." YouTube. January 7, 2002. https://www. youtube.com/watch?t=24&v=YxRcQfALqqw.

Iyengar, Sheena. "The Art of Choosing." Sheena Iyengar: The Art of Choosing | TED Talk | TED.com. July 2010. http://www.ted.com/ talks/sheena_iyengar_on_the_art_of_choosing?language=en.

Jack Ma: E-commerce in China and Around the World. Performed by Jack Ma. March 20, 2013. https://www.youtube.com/ watch?v=3OcNdxPhAUk.

Karpf, Anne. *The Human Voice: How This Extraordinary Instrument Reveals Essential Clues about Who We Are.* London: Bloomsbury Pub. Plc., 2006.

Lan, Yang. "The Generation That's Remaking China." Yang Lan: The Generation That's Remaking China | TED Talk | TED.com. Accessed February 23, 2017. http://www.ted.com/talks/yang_ lan?language=en.

LeBaron, Michelle. *Bridging Cultural Conflicts: A New Approach for a Changing World.* San Francisco, CA: John Wiley, 2004.

Livermore, David A. *Leading with Cultural Intelligence the Real Secret to Success.* New York, NY: American Management Association, 2015.

Meyer, Erin. *The Culture Map: Breaking through the Invisible Boundaries of Global Business.* New York: Public Affairs, 2014.

Miller, Casey, Kate Swift, and Kate Mosse. *The Handbook of Non-Sexist Writing for Writers, Editors, and Speakers.* London: Women's Press, 1995.

Molinsky, Andy. *Global Dexterity: How to Adapt Your Behavior Across Cultures without Losing Yourself in the Process.* Boston: Harvard Business Review Press, 2013.

Murphy, Kate. "Psst. Look Over Here." *The New York Times.* May 16, 2014. https://www.nytimes.com/2014/05/17/sunday-review/the-eyes-have-it.html.

Neeley, Tsedal. "Global Business Speaks English." *Harvard Business Review.* July 31, 2014. https://hbr.org/2012/05/global-business-speaks-english.

"Palm Up." Center for Nonverbal Studies. Accessed March 08, 2017. http://center-for-nonverbal-studies.org/htdocs/palmup.htm.

President Obama at the 2015 White House Correspondents Dinner. Performed by President Barack Obama. April 25, 2015. https://www.youtube.com/watch?v=NM6d06ALBVA.

Rogers, Todd, and Michael I. Norton. "The Artful Dodger: Answering the Wrong Question the Right Way." *Journal of Experimental Psychology: Applied* 17, no. 2 (2011): 139-47.

Scott Harrison, Founder & CEO, Charity-Water Shares His Story at LeWeb Paris 2012. Produced by Leweb.co. Performed by Scott Harrison. Vimeo. Accessed February 26, 2017. https://vimeo.com/112727142.

Strecker, Erin. "Idina Menzel Defends Her New Year's Eve Performance: 'I Am More Than the Notes I Hit.'" *Billboard.* January 5, 2015. http://www.billboard.com/articles/news/6429348/idina-menzel-defends-new-years-eve-performance.

Strunk, William, and E. B. (Elwyn Brooks) White. *The Elements of Style.* Macmillan Reference, 1962.

Thiagarajan, Sivasailam. "Mixed-Up Sentences." The Thiagi Group. January 13, 2015. http://www.thiagi.com/archived-games/2015/1/13/mixed-up-sentences.

Thoreau, Henry David. *Henry David Thoreau: Walden.* Cedar Lake, MI: ReadaClassic.com, 2010.

Wood, Aderienne. "Character & Context." How Historical Migration Patterns Shape Emotional Expression | SPSP. Accessed February 26, 2017. http://spsp.org/blog/how-historical-migration-patterns-shape-emotional-expression.

CPSIA information can be obtained
at www.ICGtesting.com
Printed in the USA
LVHW031338040821
694432LV00006B/822

9 781941 870884